Praise for *Angels by the River*

"A longtime friend and ally, Gus Speth is a tireless advocate for the environment. His accumulated stories and knowledge, the kind that could only come from decades of experience at the highest levels, provide a unique and insightful look into our history, and the way forward from here."
—Al Gore, former vice president of the United States

"Speth's story is a moving, well-told tale of transcendence: from a segregated southern town, to the forefront of the environmental struggle, to a new understanding of the deep changes we need to put our nation on a just and livable path. A critical book for change agents, young and old."
—Van Jones, author of *Rebuild the Dream* and *The Green Collar Economy*

"*Angels by the River* does what the best memoirs hope to do—launch the reader into a larger collective story. Gus Speth, a native son of the Deep South, has spent his life in the service of justice. He has not only been part of America's social and environmental history, but his leadership has helped shape it. This book is a testament to spirited engagement, showing us how 'the gift of having a cause beyond ourselves' can translate to personal and political transformation. *Angels by the River* is an antidote against despair and a prayer for action."
—Terry Tempest Williams, author of *The Open Space of Democracy*

"Gus Speth is the great environmentalist of our age, and this book chronicles not just his life's journey, but his mind's. It will make you think anew about many things, including where change comes from!"
—Bill McKibben, author of *Wandering Home* and founder of 350.org

"Gus Speth offers the gift of his own struggle to confront the systemic challenge we face as an example to anyone, young or old, seeking to find a new and possible way forward. His deeply thoughtful book is marvelous, hopeful, and above all life-affirming."
—Gar Alperovitz, cofounder of The Democracy Collaborative and author of *What Then Must We Do?*

"This book is a true gem. While guiding us through the remarkable currents of his life, Gus Speth thrills us with the breadth of his thinking and the depths of his insights. His voice is absolutely essential when it comes to the environment. And he is never less than compelling as he makes the case for transformational change on any number of other important issues, from our obsession with economic growth to US policy in the Middle East."

—Bob Herbert, distinguished senior fellow at Demos
and former op-ed columnist for the *New York Times*

"I have been fortunate to know this remarkable man, and now readers can, too. I urge you to accompany Gus Speth through his early life in the segregated South, the liberal North, the heady days of the environmental movement, and his disenchantment with inside-the-system fixes. You will find the journey engrossing, eye opening, inspiring, and deeply moving."

—Juliet Schor, cofounder of the Center for a New
American Dream and author of *True Wealth*

"You will not soon read a better or more instructive memoir—a profoundly wise reflection on a life dedicated to solving the largest challenges of our time written by an insider who grew into a radical in the best sense of the word."

—David W. Orr, counselor to the president of Oberlin College
and Steven Minter Fellow, the Cleveland Foundation

"*Angels by the River* is a personal look at the forces that shaped one of America's great environmental leaders and climate activists. Gus doesn't shy away from the dangers of climate change, but he maintains an enduring faith that people can and will make the difference. This book will engage, enlighten, and spur readers to action—just as Gus has inspired so many of us with his commitment and drive."

—Frances Beinecke, president of the
Natural Resources Defense Council

Angels by the River

Angels by the River

A MEMOIR

JAMES GUSTAVE SPETH

3 1336 09661 1752

Chelsea Green Publishing
White River Junction, Vermont

Editor: Joni Praded
Project Manager: Bill Bokermann
Copy Editor: Deborah Heimann
Proofreader: Helen Walden
Indexer: Shana Milkie
Designer: Melissa Jacobson

Printed in The United States of America.
First printing October, 2014.
10 9 8 7 6 5 4 3 2 1   14 15 16 17

Our Commitment to Green Publishing
Chelsea Green sees publishing as a tool for cultural change and ecological stewardship. We
strive to align our book manufacturing practices with our editorial mission and to reduce
the impact of our business enterprise in the environment. We print our books and catalogs
on chlorine-free recycled paper, using vegetable-based inks whenever possible. This book
may cost slightly more because it was printed on paper that contains recycled fiber, and we
hope you'll agree that it's worth it. Chelsea Green is a member of the Green Press Initiative
(www.greenpressinitiative.org), a nonprofit coalition of publishers, manufacturers, and
authors working to protect the world's endangered forests and conserve natural resources.
Angels by the River was printed on paper supplied by Thomson-Shore that contains 100%
postconsumer recycled fiber.

Library of Congress Cataloging-in-Publication Data
Speth, James Gustave.
   Angels by the river : a memoir of sorts / James Gustave Speth.
      pages cm
   Includes bibliographical references and index.
   ISBN 978-1-60358-585-9 (hardback) -- ISBN 978-1-60358-586-6 (ebook)
1. Speth, James Gustave. 2. Environmentalists--United States--Biography. 3. Civil
rights movements--Southern States--History. 4. Agriculture--Social aspects--Southern
States--History. 5. Orangeburg (S.C.)--Biography. 6. Orangeburg (S.C.)--Race relations--
History--20th century. 7. Deans (Education)--Connecticut--New Haven--Biography. 8.
Yale University. School of Forestry and Environmental Studies--Biography. 9. Radicals--
United States--Biography. 10. Social change--United States--Philosophy. I. Title.
   GE56.S69A3 2014
   363.70092--dc23
   [B]
                                   2014027808

Chelsea Green Publishing
85 North Main Street, Suite 120
White River Junction, VT 05001
(802) 295-6300
www.chelseagreen.com

For Catherine, Jim, and Charlie

Contents

Preface

I went into these woods to find myself and retrace some of the life I've lived, accounting for it along the way. I wanted to explore what became of the youngster born in the Deep South in 1942 and what became of the causes he pursued. And I sought to recapture a time and place now drifting away and to recall the people who have been the angels along the river of my life.

Often as I was writing this book, I stopped, stymied by the question: Who in the world would want to read a book about me? I have been sustained by the answer that while the pages ahead are about me, they mainly relate my personal participation in and perspective on several larger and very important developments occurring over the period since 1950. For example, I tell the story of how a group of us came together in 1970 to launch the Natural Resources Defense Council, now one of America's premier environmental organizations. And then I look beyond our founding of NRDC and address what has happened since the first Earth Day to the American environmentalism of which NRDC has been a leading part.

In this way I hope the book will be informative and helpful. America now finds itself in a sea of troubles. If we are to chart a course to a better place, we should understand how that happened. I think the stories I tell here provide insight in that exploration. I have spent a large portion of my time in recent years—talks, interviews, writings—trying to encourage others, especially young people, to join me politically at or near the place to which I have arrived, wherever they may have started. Perhaps telling the story of my journey at a more personal level will help with this encouragement.

This book is neither a comprehensive autobiography nor a memoir like many these days. Rather, it is my reflection on some past events in my life and the way those events resonate into the present—in our race relations, in the quality of our environment, in our politics, and elsewhere. Painting pictures of how these issues emerged in my life and through time—that is what I hope I have accomplished. Also, I have sought to contribute a bit to the historical record, not big history but the fine-grained perspective of one observer of events worth remembering.

Passing all of the above considerations, I have been powerfully motivated to remember and honor the amazing people in my life. Starting with family, then hometown friends, more than two decades of fellow students, a lifetime of colleagues, coconspirators, and adult friends, I have been helped and carried forward by a richness of good, loving people I did little to deserve. I cannot begin to remember them all here, but I have tried to call forth many of them.

In Part I, I describe my childhood growing up in a lovely but thoroughly segregated Southern town, Orangeburg, South Carolina. My lifelong friend Charles Tisdale says Part I is the prelude, and I think he is right. The past is indeed prologue, and these were the formative years, powerfully influencing what came later.

Then, in Part II, I tell three difficult stories. The race issue and the poison of racism are important in each. I relate what happened when I "went North" to school at Yale, then how one

South Carolina community failed to face a new civil rights reality leading in 1968 to the tragedy known as the Orangeburg Massacre, and finally how the South has proved far more successful at exporting its vices than its virtues to the rest of the country.

In order to bridge from my youth into later life and my environmental career, Part III provides a reflection on my résumé and the various jobs I've held, including how they came about. Looking back, I focus in each case on those accomplishments that seem now to be most important, and in a lighthearted way I look also at the way life's many contingencies kept me on my toes. A lot of the most interesting and telling things that happen to us don't make it into our résumés, mine included. So this chapter also looks beyond the résumé.

The trajectory of Part IV moves from the founding of NRDC and later the World Resources Institute through an analysis of what happened to American environmentalism and the specter of failure now haunting the environmental community to a discussion of my current views on what we must do as a country if we are to address our many problems, views that have earned me the label "radical" though I don't see my ideas as truly radical.

Finally, in Part V, I endeavor to relate some of the most important things I think life has taught me to date. It's short, I trust not because I have learned little.

"So we beat on," F. Scott Fitzgerald famously wrote, "boats against the current, borne back ceaselessly into the past." It is a blessing, though, to know the past, to be borne back into it. The past is passage to understanding the present and the opening to future possibility. In the chapters that follow I explore the past as one way of helping us to a better place, and I offer my thoughts on how we might now move forward to find it.

Acknowledgments

*M*uch as I am indebted to those mentioned in the chapters that follow, I am now also indebted to the wonderful group of friends, relatives, and colleagues who took the time to help me along in preparing this book. I shall always be profoundly grateful to the following people who reviewed some or all of the manuscript and helped in many ways: Richard Ayres, Jack Bass, Emerson Blake, Mary Speth Bowers, John Cavanagh, Bowman Crum, Eugenie Gentry, John Grim, Judy Albergotti Hines, Shirley Jefferson, Patti Adams Kay, Memi Speth Kinard, Pilar Montalvo, Bruce Nelson, Donna Nelson, Heather Ross, Phil Scoville, Genie Shields, Jeff Shields, Jonathan Stableford, Edward Strohbehn, and Mary Evelyn Tucker.

A special word of appreciation goes out to my friend, English professor Charles Tisdale, who read every word I gave him and commented with care and good judgment. He, like the others I mention here, bears no responsibility for any flaws or shortcomings that remain. They are mine alone.

Others, sometimes unbeknownst to them, were helpful in special ways, including James M. Albergotti III, Gar Alperovitz, Gene Atkinson, Elizabeth Billings, Ned Coffin, Roger Cohn, Elizabeth Courtney, Gordon Davis, Elizabeth Dycus, Steve Dycus, David Grant, Nancy Grant, David Korten, Sydney Lea, Kelly Levin, Therese Linehan, Don Hooper, Bill McKibben, Mason and JJ Overstreet, Pat Parenteau, Tom Powers, Will Raap, Paul

Raskin, Michael Sacca, Barbara Clark Widger, Brooke Williams, Terry Tempest Williams, and Wallace Winter.

Not enough good things can be said about Chelsea Green Publishing. President and publisher Margo Baldwin read the manuscript early on, gave me some trenchant comments, and sent me back to my writing table with encouragement and good ideas. She has guided the process throughout. My editor has been Chelsea Green senior editor Joni Praded, and she has got to be among the very finest in the business, anywhere. Her insightful guidance and coaching have been invaluable and greatly improved the manuscript. With a light touch, she has prompted me to rewrite entire chapters. To Baldwin and Praded and others at Chelsea Green, I thank you.

You will meet Cameron Council Speth in the pages that follow (known more recently as Cece since our granddaughter Cameron ran off with her name). She has worked almost as hard on this book as I have, offering up-front advice and reading and commenting on countless drafts. I would list her as coauthor, but then I couldn't get away with saying the things I do about her in the book.

To all, my deepest gratitude.

Gus Speth
Strafford, Vermont

Part I

Shall we gather at the river
Where bright angel feet have trod?

ROBERT LOWRY

ONE

The River

*T*he Edisto River rises in the sand hills of central South Carolina and glides like a glistening black snake through the Carolina lowcountry toward the coast. Its dark tannin-stained waters spread out over both banks into swamps of tall cypress, tupelo, and sweetgum draped with Spanish moss, an environment welcoming to its sunfish, heron, and the occasional alligator and water moccasin. On its way through the hardwood bottomlands and on down to the tidal marshes, the Edisto passes through Orangeburg. I was born and raised there.

I grew up in the 1940s and 1950s in that small agricultural community that was also the county seat, population 13,000. Our house was about a mile from a swimming area the town had established down from a high bluff along the Edisto. We swam there every summer. On the several terraces from the bluff's top down to the water, the girls spread blankets on the grass and worked on their (one-piece) tans. Near the riverbank, benches ran between the large cypress trees where the mothers sat watching their children play in the shallow water near the edge. A pavilion on the top of the bluff served RC Colas and hot dogs. We racked up points on the pinball machines there and listened to the juke box play "Sixty Minute Man," a song to fuel a boy's fantasy if there ever was one.

The Edisto is the river in my life. I discovered the natural world there, learned a bit about girls, learned how to swim against a current and how to dance slowly with Cameron Council in the pavilion on Friday nights after our football games.

The lovely Harriet Ann assisted in teaching us young folks how to swim and rescue, and she had one of the most beautiful figures I have ever seen. It was quite a thrill to break her choke hold, wrap one arm around her, and sidestroke her to shore. Once, to practice a longer swim, we walked through the swamp upstream to Hogpen Cove. Harriett Ann saw us all into the water, and as we waited on the sandbar on the other side of the river, she dove in. Her bathing suit strap was untied, and when she emerged from the water, it was a sight better than Sophia Loren emerging on the beach at Hydra.

One especially vivid memory of the Edisto is of drowning there. I was a preschooler, and we would jump off a platform that stuck out over the river and doggy paddle back to the ladder. I was a reckless kid, to put it mildly, and one day I got a good running start and jumped out too far, into the strength of the river's current. It carried me away fast, and soon I was underwater staring wide-eyed at the rays of sun coming through the water and completely unable to surface or gain any control. I remember thinking that I was going to drown.

Back on the benches, my dear mother, Amelia, scanned the platform area and, with alarm, said, "Where's Gus?" She and her friend Jean Jennings panicked and sprung for the river, Mom to the platform and Miss Jean for the deep water where the swimming area ended. They found me, amazingly, and I remember being wrapped up into the warm arms of two strong women and carried out of the water to the sandy bank.

I have been saved many times, and that was the first time. The Edisto is real, lovely. But the river is life itself, flowing inexorably on. The territory changes. People change. And on we go, time and the river tightly bound. Yet everywhere I have been, there have been angels along the river. They have lifted up their arms and helped me. That to me is the great mystery of this life. I have been carried forward by the caring of others. Have I repaid their caring, their gifts, grace unmerited? I pray that I have.

Except in one important respect, Orangeburg in that era was a wonderful place for a childhood. There was little crime in my world, little alcohol, no drugs, no social media, and even no TV until about the time of the Army–McCarthy hearings before Congress in 1954. Other than the bloodless cowboy movies, we were not much exposed to violence, and except for the flip-through "moving picture" booklets, there was not much porn either. But we had plenty of sports, young romance, cars and cruising, movies and drive-ins, Protestant religion, parties, hunting and fishing, and I would say, schooling. Yes, schooling. I never felt disadvantaged when I went from Orangeburg High to Yale and actually won an award for my freshman grades. And, believe me, I was no smarter than a dozen other members of the OHS Class of 1960.

I offer here two items in evidence of these points. Both were preserved for me by my mother. One is a carefully stored clipping from the Orangeburg *Times and Democrat* about a Little League baseball game in the early 1950s:

SPETH HURLS NO-HIT GAME. Gus Speth journeyed down from Boy Scout camp and hurled a no-hit game as the VFW blanked Junior Police 4 to 0 in a Little League game yesterday. The youthful pitcher almost hurled a perfect game. He allowed only one base on balls.

I boast, so let me note that I was not good at baseball, and my pitching that day may have been due to the gamma globulin shot I had just received to ward off polio. Who can say?

And regarding young romance, indeed very young, here is a note that was sent to me by a little girl whom I had met in preschool and found fetching, written in the block letter handwriting of a first grader:

Dear Gus,
   Thank you for the sweet perfume you sent me.
Cameron Council

Now, as I write this, sixty-five years after I received that nice note, Cameron Council is sitting in the room with me in our home in Vermont, poor thing, married to me for forty-nine years. Mom kept that note safe for me for over twenty years. Could she have glimpsed what was coming, or might be?

Orangeburg and the neighboring counties were heavily rural, agricultural, and poor. Sixty percent of Orangeburg County was black, and the most common livelihood for black families was farming. Cotton was still king, but for decades the boll weevil had menaced the crop, and yields were down. Poor soil management hadn't helped. Almost all those who worked the land were sharecroppers and tenant farmers. To "come a cropper" was to fall on hard times. The school year started late so that young hands could help with cotton picking. I picked cotton exactly once. It was hard work, and hot. There was some manufacturing in the area, mostly cotton gins, textile mills, meat packing, and sawmills. Reflecting the local economy, Cameron's father, Charles, was a lumberman and sawmill owner, and Daddy had a modest farm machinery business.

Our street, Middleton Street, ran from downtown out through our residential neighborhood at the edge of town where the pavement stopped, on down past a nine-hole golf course near the river, and then quickly into the country-side and its farms. When I was quite young, in the 1940s, a common sight in front of my house was a black farmer in a wooden wagon pulled by a mule headed for town. One of the mules that came by had a huge growth the size of a basketball on its hip—camel mule, I called it. Black kids would walk down Middleton regularly on weekends headed to the golf course to caddy. I became friendly with some, joking easily boy to boy, but not in a way that lasted. There was distance in these passings by, one I would not fully understand until years later.

During the decades from my childhood to 1970, I saw tremendous economic change in the area. Agriculture became more mechanized, and, for a variety of good reasons, blacks in the South moved north by the millions. The town, and indeed the whole South, devoted itself with great success to attract-ing industry, offering deep financial incentives and plentiful, cheap, and union-free labor. By the late 1960s, South Carolina had the second highest manufacturing employment per capita in the United States.

Our family—Mom and Daddy and my younger sisters Claire, Memi, and Mary—was relaxed and happy, at least after I got over my initial distress that Mary was a girl. I was a difficult child for my parents, and I will say more about that in a moment. But, all in all, the Speths actually liked and enjoyed each other, and we joked a lot. Of course we kids had lots of "fights"—nothing serious, just pushing and yelling and pulling hair. I don't recall how it started, but one time at breakfast Claire and I started throwing gobs of scrambled eggs, grits, and other breakfast foods at each other, a real food fight until we broke down in laughter. Mom was mortified.

We ate meals together often, all six of us in the dining room, not quite Norman Rockwell-like but close. Mom talked a lot more than Daddy, and these meals were commonly the occasion for her to instruct us or make a child-rearing point or two. "It's very important to show your respect for people and to thank them when they help you. Isn't that right, Gus?" she would say. And Daddy, even though he had not been listening intently, would answer, "Absolutely, Amelia." I am sure we must have heard "Absolutely, Amelia" a hundred times. Until. Until one day when Mom concluded with, "Isn't that right, Gus?" and Claire and I looked at each other and spontaneously blurted out together "Absolutely, Amelia!" The jig was up.

I respected and looked up to both my parents. They were consistently caring toward all four of us children. They loved us profoundly, and we felt that. But our family was, I must say, a somewhat laissez-faire affair. My mother and father were anything but helicopter parents, and we kids often struck out on our own. We were allowed the freedom to explore the community, find our own ways, and, inevitably, make our own mistakes. When we were a bit older, Mom and Daddy would take off on long car trips with our neighbors, Lib and John Flintom, leaving us with relatives and family friends or packing us off to summer camp.

Mom was a beautiful woman, physically and otherwise. She had a quick mind and a commanding presence. She could be tough and no nonsense, but that was softened by a real generosity, a big heart. Daddy was shorter, rounder in every way. He was thoroughly relaxed and rarely cared about his appearance. He could be very funny, and his golf and poker buddies loved him.

They were well educated. Daddy majored in history at the University of Georgia. Through some process I failed to inquire into, he then went off to get a master's degree at Cornell. His first job, during the Great Depression, was teaching math in high school in Daytona Beach, Florida, and he said he was lucky to have it. It's a long story how he ended up in the farm machinery business in Amelia's hometown, but I believe he was happy. Amelia went to Converse College and became senior class president and captain of the swimming team. "Amelia was the most beautiful girl in South Carolina," according to the reminiscences of a North Carolina legislator told to my cousin Judy Albergotti. After she got me out of her hair, she became a journalist at the Orangeburg *Times and Democrat* and in 1964 was selected as South Carolina Newspaper Woman of the Year. She was proud of that, and rightly so. Mom loved to write and was good at it. At Christmas in 1972 she gave the family a description of her childhood in Orangeburg. She wrote about the time when "progress took over and the growing village needed paved streets for the number of automobiles. The beautiful trees were cut down, and the grading, narrowing, and asphalting the streets took place. If you could look beneath the many layers of cement and tar that now cover the original paving, you would find carved for posterity the names or initials of the children marked in the soft tar, with hearts and arrows for sweethearts and ugly faces for those we were angry with on that particular day."

We lived in a modest redbrick colonial in an area called Moss Heights, and though there was a lot of Spanish moss hanging on the oaks and other trees, the neighborhood was named for the Moss family that originally owned the land. My bedroom was on the second floor, looking out at several pecan trees in the backyard. My parents, bright folks that they were, had nailed the screens in the windows closed so that I wouldn't fall out. But, early in grade school, I was even brighter. With a knife from the kitchen, I pried the nails up in the window by my bed, leaned out to yell at Claire in the yard, and, knife in hand, fell out the window. I remember being carried by Mom to the living room sofa and lying there a bit stunned. Soon thereafter my Uncle James, a doctor, arrived and pronounced me foolish but undamaged.

Years later when I was working in Washington, a reporter doing a profile on me called Mom to get some information on my childhood. She said to him, "I tell you, he was a terror." I guess she was talking about the time the police caught me trying to shoot out streetlights with my BB gun. Or maybe it was the chewed up red jelly beans I substituted for the pimentos in the olives she was serving to her bridge club or the fire I accidentally started in the woods next to our house. Or maybe it was the time I ran the hose through the window into the kitchen and turned it on, or the time my buddy Diney Young and I were caught by his father slamming .22 bullets into the pavement with slingshots to see if we could make them go off, or when we would stand on either side of Middleton Street and frighten the dickens out of oncoming cars by pretending to pull up a chain across the road. Or perhaps it was the two grade-school teachers who gave up on my deportment and asked that I be transferred to another teacher, or the fight I got into with Bobby Stokes in study hall that got me sent home, or the countless hours I spent in the principal's office or in after-school detention. Cameron's grandmother, Miss Lide, who was my next-door neighbor, thought I was "too wild" and, when the time came, advised Cameron not to go out with me.

I was an unruly cutup, regularly disobedient and in trouble, and I don't think Mom and Daddy knew what to do with me. They tried spankings and switchings, both far more psychological than physical, but I outgrew the spankings, and the switchings ended when I grabbed the switch from Mom, climbed on the bed and, pretending it was a sword, shouted, "Now *I* have the switch!" In another time and place I'm sure I would have been swooshed off to some form of behavior therapy or drug regime. I've never thought I had a problem, but I am sure I was a problem. In junior high Daddy and Mom sat me down and said that if I didn't straighten up, they were planning to pull me out of Orangeburg schools and send me off to a military academy. That truly shook me up. It was a credible threat—my friend Diney had just been shipped off to a military school in Virginia—and my behavior improved, at least for a while.

Mom loved me despite it all, as only a mother can, and she watched over my upbringing. In high school, I did my homework in the early mornings, and Mom was always up with me, ready to help. She pointed me to some great reads: Caldwell's *Dear and Glorious Physician*, de Kruif's *Microbe Hunters*, Michener's *The Bridges at Toko-ri*, Waltari's *The Egyptian*, Costain's *The Silver Chalice*, and more. Far more than school, that guidance launched a lifetime of reading. I am not too proud to admit that I also plowed through volume after volume of *Reader's Digest Condensed Books*.

One day a small group came to our front door promoting some good social cause; I cannot remember what. I answered the knock and got very engaged in talking with them on the front steps. From the living room I heard Daddy say, "Amelia, could you tell them thanks and to move on?" Her reply was revealing: "Let him talk with them. We shouldn't diminish his idealism." And they didn't. I was raised to be optimistic and hopeful and to believe the world could be a better place, and I will always be grateful for that.

Orangeburg had a good supply of my mother's relatives. Our cousins, the three Albergotti kids, lived a block farther out Middleton Street from us, where the pavement ended. Their ages were about the same as ours, and we were close to them. Their father, James Albergotti, Mom's brother, was a pediatrician, and he was our doctor growing up. Uncle James saw me often in his practice, sewing me up with some regularity, and he helped me with science fair projects, including finding the vagus nerve in the throat of a bullfrog. Once he dropped by our house and told me he was giving me a subscription to *American Heritage*, then a hardbound periodical and amazingly beautiful. "You have enough sense to benefit from it," he said.

The River

One visit to Uncle James's office was especially memorable. In junior high, my neighbor Watty Stroman and I had ridden bikes to the movie downtown, a couple of miles away. But these were no ordinary bikes. They had small, thin tires and hand-brakes, and they peddled backward. We called them English bikes, and Watty and his sister Snooky had just gotten them. I was riding Snooky's bike, my first time on an English bike. After what was likely a double feature of cowboy movies—perhaps a Lash LaRue and a Red Ryder—we headed home. On a nice downhill stretch, I decided it would be fun to go free wheeling down the Broughton Street centerline, and at some point I realized that the bike was moving too fast, whizzing by cars and trucks on both sides, and that I was headed straight for a truck coming up the hill. So, in a panic, I instinctively slammed on the foot brakes and thus pedaled backward into Caroline Williams's father's oncoming pickup. The bike was totaled but, more important I guess, I took the full force of the collision on my head and face. After I came to in Uncle James's office, Mom arrived, and when I smiled at her, she almost fainted because most of my front teeth were gone, broken off at the gums, never to return. Beyond the teeth, I have often wondered what other damage that head injury caused.

Orangeburg had its full share of parades, costume parties, talent shows, and other festivities, and we Speth kids would collaborate with the Albergottis, together becoming a wedding party or a chain gang. When she was five, Memi was Queen of the Edisto. The town sponsored water parades with actual floats proceeding with the current down the river. Queen Memi and her king, the handsome little Carl Mutch, both decked out in white satin, waved to their subjects along the bank, and came away with the prize for best float.

Granny and Granddaddy, Claire and Jim Albergotti, lived closer to downtown in a neighborhood of impressive older homes. They were an inspiration, she with her garden and he with his Harvard Classics almost fully read. They convened big family dinners at Christmas, Thanksgiving, and New Year's Day, their wedding anniversary. During high school, I visited with Granddaddy most weeks, often on Sunday afternoon. We talked about serious matters, including the books he was reading. Once, when I was home from college, I asked him where his loyalties were—the United States, the South, or South Carolina. He answered, "In exactly that order, but in reverse."

Mr. Jim, as Granddaddy was known, had done well as a cotton broker. Wiped out in the Great Depression, he recouped his fortunes after World War II and became a major contributor to civic improvements in town. They had a second home at the

The Speth Family. *From left*: Memi, Gus, Mary, Amelia, Claire, and the author.

lovely Methodist retreat center on Lake Junaluska in the North Carolina mountains, and I would spend two or three weeks each summer with them there.

Granny was a prim and proper lady, a little strict with those around her but basically very nice. She could laugh at herself and was fond of telling about the time she and her fellow garden club members were driving to Columbia for a show. Dressed to the nines and donning summer bonnets, they were in two 1920s cars, moving slowly with all the windows down on a hot day, when they encountered the dusty chain gang working on the road. As they slowed to creep over the rubble, one of the chain gang members stuck his head in the car window and loudly said, "Good morning, cousin Claire! I hope you have a fine day." It was indeed that Salley cousin, embarrassing her in front of all her friends.

Of course, it was not all roses. Growing up I saw a lovely mother of a friend stumble around their house and finally kill herself with alcohol and a brilliant medical doctor lose his ability to practice thanks to an affection for his own narcotics. My strong Granny became "senile" in her late seventies and began to verbally attack Granddaddy, reducing him to tears Mom said. Daddy lost his mother in 1945, his sister Mable Claire to a heart attack in 1947 when she was only forty-five years old, and his father, Grandpop, who had come to live with us, passed away in 1950. In five years his whole family was gone. But nothing compares to the tragedy that hit our family much later, in 1988, when my sister Claire, by then the mother of three, was killed in one of those interstate highway calamities involving dozens of vehicles. A cloudbank caused by a nearby chemical plant had simply blinded them all. Our family carried on, but we were deeply wounded. Death happens, but sometimes it shouldn't.

It was good of Mom and Daddy to invite Grandpop to come live with us. But he was very set in his ways, and it was a strain for Mom, dealing with him and raising four children. He loved fried grits and cornbread—not that cakelike concoction we see today but real cornbread, dry and demanding. We rarely ate either after he died. Grandpop loved to fish, was good at it, and did a lot of it, but his real love was his big maroon station wagon with actual wood trim outside and inside. Earlier in his life he had developed and sold a car wax, and he kept that baby beautiful. He made me pray each night, kneeling beside my bed. I never did that before or since. One time he said to me, "Son, one day you will either be president or in jail." Turns out, he had that just about right. And then as quickly as he came, he was gone. He was a second generation German American and the first in a line of five Speths born on these shores to be named Gustave, so far.

We had windows into other, more difficult lives but as children didn't see through them, at least not right away. Cora Fogle and then Maggie Bowman worked for our family as maids for a total of about forty-five years. Cora was big and bold, larger than life. She smoked a pipe, and, yes, she kept her hair in a dozen little braids that she covered with a kerchief. Maggie was shy and gentle, one of the sweetest people I've known. They helped to raise me, and I loved them both. In 1971 Maggie wrote me a gracious thank you note for a present I had given her. She addressed it "To the nicest man in the world: my Gus Speth." Overstated, to be sure, but I have treasured it. Cora saved my life or at least our house when she carried the flaming bedding and mattress I had set on fire (playing with matches) into the bathroom and turned on the shower. She also badly burned her arms. I am told that I had crawled under the flaming bed. Maggie became the caregiver to Mom in her long struggle with emphysema. After Mom died in 1991, Memi and Mary stayed in touch with Maggie, and we continued to pay her a modest salary until she passed away. Both Cora and Maggie had children. It never occurred to me that they were spending more time with the Speth children than with their own families.

One day I wanted to buy a present for Cora, just to give her something nice to show my affection. I knew she and her family were poor, but, in grade school at the time, I was too unaware to associate that with the low pay she and other domestic workers received from folks like us. I got on my bike that day and pedaled up to the Hillcrest Drug Store, which was about a half mile from our house, and I bought her some tobacco. Cora laughed and hugged me when I gave the tobacco to her. Then slowly she let me know, in case I might be prepared to do something like that again or maybe just to tease me, that the tobacco I had bought was chewing tobacco, not pipe tobacco. What did I know! The next time I did better.

When we were small, my sisters and I were also looked after by two teenagers, Colman and Ernestine from the Davis family. Like Cora and Maggie, they were black. They lived in a very poor area only blocks from us called Sunnyside. Colman was around a lot taking care of me, and he joined us to visit my aunt, Mable Claire, and her husband, Robert Hand, at their beautiful farm near Plainfield, New Jersey. Colman was good to me, and I looked up to him. Ernestine took care of Claire and Memi and impressed Mom with her brightness and dedication to her schoolwork. I recall her always having her schoolbooks with her. Mom mentioned several times that she wanted to help Ernestine continue her education, and indeed I learned later that Mom offered to send her to college. But Ernestine, with her new husband and baby, headed north instead. Decades later an attractive, well-dressed black woman knocked on Mom's front door one Christmas when our whole family was there. Ernestine had come to visit, especially to see Mom.

I mentioned that there was one important respect in which Orangeburg was flawed, and some flaw it was. Our region was in the lowcountry, but it was also in the Black Belt. In 1950, as I mentioned, Orangeburg County was 60 percent African American, and the county's schools, neighborhoods, restrooms, public accommodations, water fountains, toilets, restaurants, lunch counters, churches, theaters, recreational facilities, and social life were all thoroughly segregated. The town maintained two swimming beaches on the Edisto, one for whites and one for blacks. It is not hard to guess which was downstream. The races were separate and certainly not equal. Disparities in income, health, education, longevity, job opportunity—indeed, opportunities of all sorts—were huge, gaping.

Segregation did not preclude a multitude of face-to-face interactions between blacks and whites. Most downtown businesses catered to both races. Black people and white people often worked side by side, including at the Carolina Equipment Company and Council Wood Products. And most middle-class white families, like ours, employed black maids and nursemaids and other help—cooks, caddies, and yardmen. In these ways and others, the races were constantly interacting personally. Though there were big walls, and do's and don'ts, black people and white people were certainly not strangers to each other. In my experience, these interactions were mostly friendly and, within the confines of the system, respectful. However, that system itself was thoroughly demeaning, and we white people were hugely dependent on the support, labor, and subservience of black people. When I was growing up, I saw lots of prejudice and discrimination directed at blacks, but I saw little hate or violence. That was not every Southern white boy's experience, and surely not the black experience. As I describe in the chapter that follows, I eventually recognized and confronted my own prejudice, but that did not happen in Orangeburg. Perhaps I would have awakened earlier to the massive injustice all around me had I been exposed to racial cruelty rather than sheltered from it. Perhaps had there been some real questioning and open debate in the white community, I would have chosen wisely. I would like to think so, but I'll never know.

It is a strange thing to think of how where you have been carries you to where you are, whether you know it or not along the way. I was baptized James Gustave Speth Jr. in 1942 in the restrained Episcopal manner, not the full dousing that Cameron got as a First Baptist. I thus became Little Gus, and remained that for far too long. Daddy was Big Gus, and his small farm machinery business—remembered fondly by me in part for the large Marilyn Monroe calendar that told the dates year after year—focused heavily on repairing harrows and keeping worn-out tractors running. We were one of the few families to welcome hurricane season, for Daddy would leave the shop (telephone number 315) and for a few weeks take up claims adjusting for insurance companies. Our family income was not large—about $10,000 to $12,000 a year—but we did not feel deprived or lacking in anything. We felt secure in our lives in the community. It helped, perhaps, that Mom's grandfather had been mayor for many years. There were people in town with more money, for sure, but Orangeburg was not a place for ostentatious displays. Memi has said to me, "We did not know we were not rich." It is a cliché, I know, but we were rich in the ways that counted.

The customers of the Carolina Equipment Company often lacked the cash to pay their bills and so paid in the products of their labors. Sometimes this was bootleg whiskey, and Daddy stored the moonshine in the men's room at the shop—small wooden kegs stacked to the ceiling. One never knew when a batch would end up methanol rather than ethanol, but for some reason it was kept and stored, until one day the bottom keg burst open from the sheer weight on it and flooded out "all over everything," Big Gus reported.

Daddy allowed the town to keep the DDT truck in the yard at the shop. My buddies and I loved to follow the DDT truck on our bikes as it roamed through residential neighborhoods, spraying for mosquitoes. Our goal was to see if we could become invisible by getting deep into the white spray it blew all over everything. I am full of DDT.

Prior to his discovery of golf in the late 1950s, Daddy's passions were hunting and fishing. I was his companion on many of these outings and by junior high had my own shotgun. His specialty was jigger fishing for redbreast and bream on the Edisto. Jigger fishing was its own art, and not just for the fisherman. It required not only the right cane pole but also a skilled paddler to move the wooden flat-bottomed boat at just the right speed and into just the right places. That was certainly not me, but one Gene Browder. Whenever Browder's name came up, Amelia knew she would lose Big Gus for a day, but at least she'd be done for a while with the catawba worms he kept in the fridge for bait.

My hunting trips with Daddy were the occasion for one of my most embarrassing moments as well as one of my greatest accomplishments, at least by my lights as a young boy. The dove hunt is a Southern tradition. A farmer would leave a modest amount of corn and soybeans in the field, and early on the day of the hunt someone would scare the mourning doves out of the field. In the afternoon, with the doves eager to return, the invited guests would move into the field, build cornstalk blinds for themselves, and wait for the doves to fly in. Doves are quite tasty.

I had better get the bad news done first. On a fine fall day in 1956 when I was fourteen, I was walking into the field with another hunter, a farmer about my father's age, and he asked me, "Do you want a chaw?," offering me his block of chewing tobacco. Being the man I surely was, I took a generous bite. We proceeded into the field in slightly different directions—the blinds should not be too close to each other. Very soon I realized my mouth was full of tobacco juice, my cheeks were like a chipmunk's, and I began to wonder what I was supposed to do next. My conclusion was that the proper thing to do was to swallow the juice. So I did. Within a second or two my world started spinning, I was nauseated, and then, BLAM! my gun went off. It flew out of my hands, and, too dizzy to stand, I fell into the dirt. As I was lying there with the world twirling around, the shotgun several feet away, I looked up at the same farmer standing over me, who said, "Are you all right?" I tried to explain what happened, and he said, "You shot me, but I'm okay." At a sufficient distance birdshot will bounce off a canvas hunting jacket, or, if it hits the skin, it, as the farmer said, "stings a bit." Why was the gun's safety not on?

On another hunt, around that same time, Daddy and I and several others were walking together out of the field as dusk was approaching, the hunt over. The birds were either in the bag or in the trees. But one last dove entered the field at the far end, flying high, and someone yelled, "Mark!" All of us still in the field dropped to one knee and waited to see where the bird would head. It flew toward our group, and when it was overhead but almost too high to shoot at, Daddy said, "Take it, Gus." So I stood and fired my 20 gauge, leading the bird more than a bit, and, amazingly, it fell to our feet. Daddy was very proud of me that day.

I was too, then. But I see it differently now. The beautiful mourning doves enjoy the sunflower seeds under our bird feeders here in Vermont. They gather and rest on ledges and make their sounds, not all mournful. They sit on our windowsill and look in at me with their big black eyes, and I hope they are saying they hold no grudges.

I was not raised an environmentalist. My parents did not talk of nature or conservation. Growing up I did not even know a bird-watcher. But the natural world was all around me, in healthy shape, and taken for granted. I did hunt, and I did fish. And I swam in the Edisto and followed beagles through the woods looking for rabbits. It was Diney Young's beagle mostly, and he taught me that once the rabbit was on chase, as often as not it would circle back to where it started. So we would go to that spot, find a stump to stand on, and wait. I became a Life Scout, and I hiked in the Philmont Scout Ranch in New Mexico, and I was amazed there. I did not know the concept of wilderness, but I knew a lot of wild places.

On a dare late one night, I stripped and floated the Edisto from the final rope across the swimming area for a half mile down to the US 301 bridge. I remember it was very peaceful, drifting with the current, unable to see much of anything in the darkness of the Edisto river swamp near midnight.

For several summers around junior high years I went to visit Granny and Granddaddy at their house on Lake Junaluska, tucked in a region between Asheville and the Great Smokies. Their house looked across the lake to Mount Junaluska. I swam in the lake and took Granddaddy's small boat into every corner of it. But I began to notice things I had not noticed in Orangeburg. A strong odor hung over the community many mornings, a smell I did not know. They explained to me it was the paper mill at Canton. Once we were driving along the French Broad River and I noticed the water had a strange color and was foaming. When I asked about it, Granddaddy said it was the result of the rayon plant at Enka. And then one year I arrived at Lake Junaluska to find that the whole, beautiful 200-acre lake had been contaminated and closed to swimming. It was brown and smelly. Dead. I was told that a company had dumped its wastes into the lake, a tanning operation I think. I was devastated. Environmental seeds were planted at Lake Junaluska, I'm sure of that, and planted also when I went north in 1960 and saw pollution everywhere. The contrast with home was jarring. It wasn't just pollution that I discovered at Lake Junaluska. It was also the sources of the pollution—large companies like Champion Paper and American Enka. I was beginning to connect the dots.

Though I was an Episcopalian, I still took religion seriously. Cameron and I argued frequently over whether the Baptists or the Episcopalians had it right. Regardless, if I wanted to go out with her on Sunday nights, first I had to join her family for the Sunday evening service at the First Baptist Church on the square downtown. The Reverend Bill Lancaster, a great preacher, was pastor. That was when I discovered singing hymns. They sang songs like:

> *I was sinking deep in sin,*
> *Far from the peaceful shore,*
> *Very deeply stained within*
> *Sinking to rise no more.*

Meanwhile, we Episcopalians were struggling to find the tune:

> *Now, my tongue, the mystery telling*
> *Of the glorious Body sing,*
> *And the Blood, all price excelling...*

The Baptists had the Bible, but we had the Book of Common Prayer. I treasured it, my first literature. Consider the Confession: "Almighty God, Father of our Lord Jesus Christ, maker of all things, judge of all men; we acknowledge and bewail our manifold sins and wickedness, which we, from time to time, most grievously have committed, by thought, word, and deed, against thy divine majesty, provoking most justly thy wrath and indignation against us. We do earnestly repent, and are heartily sorry for these our misdoings; the remembrance of them is grievous unto us; the burden of them is intolerable. Have mercy upon us. . . ."

And the Nicene Creed: " . . . the only-begotten Son of God; begotten of his Father before all worlds, God of God, Light of Light, Very God of Very God; begotten, not made; being of one substance with the Father, by whom all things were made; who for us men and for our salvation came down from heaven and was incarnate by the Holy Ghost of the Virgin Mary, and was made man. . . ."

Magnificent, whether or not you believe it!

I was an altar boy and a good one. I would don vestments with The Reverend Thomas Sumter Tisdale and was so proud to join him at the altar of the Church of the Redeemer and assist with Holy Communion. I loved the words, the ritual, the belonging, the sense of something beyond and better, but I do not think I ever thought there was a God active in the world, listening to my prayers—at least I did not take that very seriously. I never believed there were signs from God, and God was just too abstract to actually love. But I did love Camp St. Christopher.

As the Edisto becomes tidal and enters the Atlantic, it splits north and south around Edisto Island. The north branch flows by Seabrook Island, like Edisto a coastal barrier island near Charleston. Seabrook had been given to the Episcopal Diocese of South Carolina by the Morawetz family with the requirement that its natural beauty remain unspoiled, and Camp St. Christopher was the only thing on it. I went there as a camper for many summers. First as a camper and later as a counselor, I got to know a group of seminarians and young ministers, and discussing theology with them was the most intellectually exciting thing I did as a boy. I became a leader in the diocese-wide Youth Commission, and organized a silent retreat and other events for the state's young people. Then I went off to Yale, and I lost interest in organized religion, stopped going to church, and, down the road a bit, realized that I had become an atheist of a sort. How all that happened so quickly, and after such a good start, I am not at all sure. Perhaps I will find Jesus as the Grim Reaper closes in on me. It has been known to happen.

The sunsets at Camp St. Christopher, looking northwest back up the Edisto, the loggerhead turtles coming ashore to lay their eggs, the pluff mud up to your knees in the saltmarsh with the fiddler crabs scurrying about—it will always be with me. If I had been raised a pantheist, I might still be one. Perhaps I am.

Years later the Diocese, contrary to the Morawetz deed, would sell most of Seabrook to developers. As Faulkner said in *Go Down, Moses*, the very act of selling the land should have forfeited the seller's claim to it.

My final stay at Camp St. Christopher was in June 1960, right after graduating from Orangeburg High School. We were pleased to have our bishop, Thomas Carruthers, join us. The bishop was a large man in every way—size, presence, booming voice—and clearly enjoying himself with us young people. One evening we hiked for a mile down the mouth of the Edisto and around the point onto Seabrook's pristine front beach and had a cookout there. Afterward, the bishop, staff in hand, led us back to the camp's cabins.

The bishop went to his room in the counselors' cabin, and I joined a small group of young ministers on the cabin's porch. They were talking and I was listening when we heard a loud thud from the bishop's room. It sounded ominous, and we all rushed to his door. Through the door we could hear the bishop snoring, and when we tried to open the bedroom door it was clear something was holding it shut on the other side. At this point, one of the ministers said that the bishop had been complaining about his door banging in the wind, so he must have blocked it shut with a suitcase. Another added that he had been complaining about being tired and after the hike must have gone quickly to sleep. So we moved quietly back to the porch and resumed our conversation. Later that night, back in my cabin, I would learn that the bishop, age sixty, had died that evening of a cerebral hemorrhage. He had fallen against his door, and snoring is common in such incidents. I felt terrible that we might have been able to help him. True or not, I was assured that it was already too late. I learned then never to underestimate the power of the human mind to deny unpleasant realities.

Immediately before reaching Seabrook Island, the Edisto passes by the settlement known as Rockville, a small gathering of very old homes and very large live oak trees. It is a beautiful spot from a long lost era and is best known today for its sailing regatta. My good buddy from Beaufort, Mike Jones, sailed his moth in all the coastal regattas, and one summer during my high school years, when Gus and Amelia and John and Lib had disappeared on one of their road trips, Mike signed me on as his crew. Moths have no actual crew, tiny one-person boats that they are, but it got me into all the parties, including the famous one at Rockville, held after the race every August since 1890.

The Rockville clubhouse was (and still is) a modest one-story clapboard structure in the lowcountry style, with a large open floor for dancing. Its huge windows and porch on multiple sides made the whole thing veranda-like when opened up. The band was great that night; the dance floor was crowded, mostly with young people; it was hot; and the alcohol was flowing. As I walked outside to cool off, I saw in the dark corners a truly serious amount of petting and such and noticed couples headed for the backseats of the parked cars. Feeling especially lonely after missing out on what was very close to a drunken orgy, I sat on one of the porch benches next to two well-dressed matronly women. Despite the loud music, I could not help but overhear their conversation. The lady next to me said in a charming Charleston accent, "This event has gone terribly downhill." "Yes," the other agreed, "What a shame that the young men are dancing without their jackets!"

The disciplinary problems of my younger years persisted into my freshman year at OHS. I am quite unclear what would have become of me had I continued on the path I was on. Perhaps I would have accomplished little in later life. I know I was embarrassing Mom, who was teaching English at OHS at the time. Yet she had become as much a friend as a mother, and she stuck with me. We talked a lot. I had been elected a freshman class officer, but my class dumped me sophomore year, not electing me to anything. That got my attention.

At some point when we were sophomores at OHS, Cameron and I started going steady, and we have been together ever since. She was a beautiful creature then and that's true today, too: high-spirited, steady, happy, and, as her father Charles would say, she has the charm to tease the lard out of a biscuit. Dating Cameron also helped get me on a better track. It has been said that Gus settled down after he started going with Cameron Council, a development that Mom quietly promoted. Mom and Cameron, the archangels of my life.

Looking back, I can see that I was saved by love and politics. In sophomore year, I stopped being a "bad example for

Cameron Council, junior year, Orangeburg High.

the students," and worked hard at becoming a good one. The
residue of my accumulated misbehavior is a nagging sense of
guilt, a conscience that won't quit, still with me. I have tried to
put it to good use, to do positive things. "The child is father to
the man," as Wordsworth wrote.

Junior year, both Cameron and I ran for student body president. The way the election was conducted required a runoff

between the boy and the girl with the most votes. The winner of the runoff would be president and the loser vice-president. The boy had always won, but there was no guarantee (and indeed that would soon change). Well, Cameron and I won the first round, and so we squared off against each other in the runoff. I'm not sure my ego could have survived had I lost. Cameron was more popular than I, and I have always thought she was determined not to win. Even today she won't confess she threw the election, but I can see her telling her friends to vote for Gus. I did win, and we were a good pair and performed our school duties with care. I'm sure being student body president helped get me into Yale, and, as we shall see, that turned out to be very important in this story.

Sports were important at OHS. Senior year proved that it was possible for the student body president to sit on the bench throughout the entire varsity basketball season. I was better at football and was first string for two years at right guard and linebacker. I was also on the varsity sophomore year, until I executed the perfect tackle in a practice scrimmage. Our 220-pound fullback was coming straight at me. I leveled into his stomach, wrapped my arms around the back of his knees, lifted him onto my shoulder, and started to drive him back. The next thing I knew I was flat on my back and his metal cleats were driving across my body. One resulted in a six-inch gash along my left shin, and I was soon in the hospital and out for the season. There's an ugly scar there to this day.

The fact that I did not follow doctor's orders and was back on the field next season led to the time I made Daddy proudest. To my surprise, honestly, I was awarded the school's trophy for combining athletics, scholarship, and leadership. Big Gus just sat there in the gym full of all his friends and other members of the OHS booster club beaming, while I was too shocked to figure out what to say. Mom was proud of me too, but in a different way. She said to me one day, "Son, you are not great at anything, but you are very good at many things." I won't argue with that.

I am sure the person behind that award was W. J. "Bill" Clark, a teacher and our football coach. Nicknamed the Gray Fox, Clark's lifetime coaching record was 133 wins, 37 losses, and 12 ties—amazing since little Orangeburg played many of the largest high schools in the state. He was an impressive man, a hero in World War II, Gregory Peck handsome, smart, and charismatic but always approachable and helpful. I respected him greatly, and he counted on me as defensive captain. Football with Bill Clark actually did teach me all the clichéd things—the importance of teamwork, of playing fair, of perseverance, of punching above your weight, of preparation, of appreciating a crowd of supporters cheering you on. To this day, when I am on grass, I often want to drop into a three-point stance and charge forward, though it would finish off what's left of my back. As I try to drift off to sleep, I find myself reliving plays, pulling down the line to trap block, intercepting passes, and Clark coaching, always coaching. Bill Clark will return to this story some years later, as he tried with Reverend Tisdale to lead Orangeburg in the right direction on the civil rights issue.

All this would somehow lead to Yale, a journey that began one day in the fall of 1959 when Mom said, "It's time to talk about college, son."

"Yes, Mom."

"I want you to go to one of America's great colleges," she said.

"Which are the best?"

"Harvard, Princeton, and Yale," she answered.

"In that order?"

"No. And I don't want you to go to Harvard," she said firmly.

"Why?"

"The foreign element is too strong there," and she and I left it at that.

So I applied to Princeton, Yale, Davidson, and, because I wanted to be a scientist, MIT as well. I was admitted to all four, but because Yale's scholarship was by far the most generous, I went to Yale. It was just that simple, except for one thing. Yale sent us a form, and among other things, it asked about preferences in roommates. Mom said, "In that space, put 'I prefer to room with someone of my own, Caucasian, race.'" So I did, and Yale obliged, but it was easy for them to do so. There were not many non-Caucasians in the Yale Class of 1964.

Mom was certainly among the most open-minded, unprejudiced people I knew in Orangeburg. She steered me away from Harvard and into a suite full of white guys at Yale, but it was she who sent me up north to a Yankee school and a liberal environment. She knew what she was doing. She wanted to protect her boy from aspects of a world she had never seen, but she knew there was a larger, more progressive world out there, and she wanted me to be part of it.

Of the four schools, nearby Davidson was the only one I visited before deciding. I don't remember much about Davidson, but I remember well the student who was assigned to show me around—one Henry Shue, who would go on to become a distinguished philosopher in political theory and human rights. I recall Henry vividly because from our first encounter he began to challenge me on race and segregation. I don't believe I had said anything to prompt the subject, but that did not matter. Henry lectured me about the need for racial justice. I think I just looked bewildered. No one had ever pushed me so hard in that direction before, and it made me think.

One reason I thought I might do well at Yale was that I believed I had received a good education in the public schools of Orangeburg, especially in science and math. The OHS science fair project I did with my friend Bowman Crum carried us all the way to an award at the National Science Fair in Indianapolis, Indiana, and in 1959, during my junior year, I was selected to participate in a National Science Foundation summer program at the New Mexico Institute of Mining and Technology. So my hat is off to OHS's Doc Moore who had a crippling disease that left him straight as a board from his neck to his feet but who brilliantly taught us math up through calculus, to Sudie Bonnette who introduced me to a foreign language and culture, to Mason Turner who skillfully showed us the internal logic and beauty of the periodic table, to Lucille McComb who drilled us on grammar and *Silas Marner*, to OHS principal Gene Smith who hired only the best and made us students feel special about ourselves. They and many others devoted their lives to us and did so for about $3,200 a year, with little recognition and insufficient appreciation.

When Mom and Daddy and I arrived at Phelps Gate at Yale in September 1960, Mom looked around Yale and New Haven for the first time, and this is what she said: "I think Yale means more to New Haven than the University of South Carolina means to Columbia." Smart lady.

Mom and Daddy put my bags on the curb, gave me big hugs and kisses, and drove away. I can only imagine the things they must have thought as they left me there. Nothing would ever be the same. All the good times we'd had and all the difficulties I'd caused. But it had ended well, and I think they were happy.

They had left me at Yale, on the Old Campus, and somewhere through Phelps Gate was 35 Vanderbilt Hall.

Cameron and I continued to go together through our college years. She went to Coker College in Hartsville, South Carolina. It was a long way from Yale, but we would both head home to Orangeburg during breaks and for the summers. I avoided the Yale mixers with the Seven Sisters, and I had no dates, not a one, while at Yale, except when Cameron would come to visit once each year. It was such a joy to see her get off the train in New Haven. But we will never forget her last such visit. She arrived on Thursday, November 21, 1963. The Harvard–Yale game was scheduled for the twenty-third, but on Friday President Kennedy was assassinated in Dallas. It was a somber weekend, to say the least.

After graduation, during the summer of 1964 as I was getting ready to head for Balliol College, Oxford, on my Rhodes Scholarship, I asked Cameron to go to Columbia with me to get a new setting for Mom's engagement ring. When we got to the jewelry store, my cover story seemed to have worked because Cameron seemed quite surprised when I said we were there to get it fitted for her finger. Of course, I had to rush back to Orangeburg to ask Cameron's father, Charles, for permission to marry his daughter.

And so it came to pass that on July 3, 1965, Cameron and I were married in the First Baptist Church, packed with all our friends in Orangeburg, Reverends Lancaster and Tisdale jointly officiating. The next day we flew to Europe for our honeymoon. I had smoked my last cigarette in the vestibule of the church, as Daddy and I waited together for the wedding ceremony to begin. Cameron would soon conclude that quitting was the right thing at the wrong time. She says I was entirely too irritable on our honeymoon, trying to pilot our VW Bug from England to Istanbul and back.

Shortly after, a fascinating thing happened. Daddy decided that he had seen enough to conclude he'd been wrong about some things on the race issue. I'm not saying he became a champion of integration, but his views became increasingly moderate, and when the opportunity presented itself, he became the director of the Orangeburg Community Action Program, part of the federal Office of Equal Opportunity. Who could have imagined: Big Gus, working with a predominantly black staff and leading the war on poverty in Orangeburg! I asked him once what he said when his conservative friends questioned him about his new life. He answered, "Real friends will stay real friends, and, besides, I tell them I'm getting all my taxes back." Daddy and I had some strong discussions on the segregation issue, and he once had an argument that grew quite heated with several of my fraternity brothers who we had as houseguests as they were driving to join the civil rights protests in Mississippi. But I think he was moved more by civil rights events in the country than anything else.

In 1969, a few months before the Chesterfields finally got Daddy, I walked into our darkened den and he was watching Spencer Tracy struggling to bring his big fish to shore in *The Old Man and the Sea*. His heart was already failing and his deeply lined face was wet with tears. It was a time of endings, and I sat on the sofa with him, close. I knew I might not see him again after that break from law school and that turned out to be the case. The South Carolina OEO director Lee Spratt wrote this about him in a eulogy: "More than my missing Gus, his people in his counties are going to feel his absence, his staff, his agency, and the poor people with whom he worked. . . . One thing Gus had going for him was his genuine sense of honesty and forthrightness. He wasn't one to mince words. . . . Aside from all this, he was a hellava lot of fun to be with at a party. No one enjoyed a good time more than Gus."

———————

As I have related, I had numerous encounters with the Grim Reaper growing up. But there is one narrow escape that happened in high school when I was old enough to know better.

I had spent some time in Beaufort, South Carolina with Mike Jones, he of the moth sailboat, and my family often spent summer vacations on Edisto Island, up the coast from Beaufort toward Charleston, where the south branch of the Edisto flows into the Atlantic. It occurred to me that it would be exciting to take a boat and go from the Beaufort area across St. Helena Sound to Edisto Beach! Two of my best high school friends, Bowman Crum and Phil Scoville, were up for the adventure, so I asked Daddy if I could take his fishing boat to knock around on the coast for a couple of days. He agreed and later told me it was one of his dumbest decisions. The boat was a small, shallow draft 12-footer with a 15 horsepower outboard—a lake boat.

As any good map will show, St. Helena Sound is huge, basically open ocean. When we started out the weather seemed calm, but that quickly changed. The wind picked up, the clouds lowered, the swells grew, but on we went, determined to make it across. I was in the rear, steering the small motor. When we were a good ways out, perhaps a third of the way, the wind strengthened and a light rain began, so that we could barely see land. Soon the swells grew so large that when we'd ride up on one, the motor would come clean out of the water and rev up with a ferocious roar. Daddy's boat, like Snooky's bike, was getting out of control. There were no life vests aboard, and I was pretty sure we were going to die out there. I've never felt before or after the sense of dread that I felt then. Phil and Bowman were huddled in the front having the same thought. Back in Orangeburg, Daddy heard about the storm that had come ashore between Charleston and Beaufort and started worrying. Belatedly, I decided to maneuver between the swells to turn the boat around and head back toward Beaufort. I remember the total relief I felt as the waters calmed when we approached some misty piece of undeveloped land on the Beaufort side of the sound, possibly Morgan Island. Bowman and Phil started joking around and teasing each other; anxiety lifted. We camped there that night, and the next morning, weather calm, we set out again for Edisto Beach. How could we have done that rather than find the nearest church and throw ourselves before the altar shivering and stammering!

Other than confirm for me my own mortality and potential for recklessness, my string of narrow escapes likely confirmed the risk taker in me. There's a certain confidence born of making risky decisions and coming out okay. In any case, I survived my youth and lived on to have a career, duly recounted in my résumé, beginning with an impressive higher education and then one good job after another. I will discuss that résumé a little later, including some things it does not report.

As for the Edisto River, it is still beautiful, still the longest free-flowing blackwater river in North America. The swimming area is abandoned and the sand beach is grown over with wetland vegetation. The ropes, platforms, diving board, and benches are gone. But the river is still a great sight. Cameron and I return to it often, looking down from the bluff through the bald cypress near the banks to the memories of floating down the cold waters from Rocky Bottom around the bend to the end of the swimming area. It is a fine spot for standing and remembering, a sacred place. And we are twice-blessed to have been raised as we were and to have found each other.

Part II

To change is not necessarily to lose one's identity,
to change sometimes is to find it.

GEORGE TINDALL

TWO

Things Fall Apart

*I*t can be frightening when the old myths, orthodoxies, the settled ways of thinking are threatened or even stripped bare, and we are left without their aid to confront big questions of who we really are, what we can or should believe, and, in various forms, what survives. Something very much like that happened to countless whites in the South during the civil rights revolution, myself included, and many different paths were taken in that epochal period, some more commendable than others. My path through the thicket began at Yale, but the story begins in Orangeburg.

I have only a limited idea of what it was like to grow up black in Orangeburg. But I have a reliable source who had that experience, an Orangeburg native son, the Pulitzer-winning journalist Eugene Robinson. In his insightful book, *Disintegration: The Splintering of Black America*, he comments briefly about growing up in Orangeburg.[1] Born in 1955, Robinson lived in Orangeburg during what he called the "last throes" of Jim Crow. His experience was atypical in some ways and not in others.

He wrote, "When I was growing up in the late 1950s and early 1960s, my own private black America was essentially a college town. Orangeburg, South Carolina, is home to two historically black colleges, Claflin University and South Carolina State University, which sit side by side just a couple of hundred yards from the house, built by my great-grandfather, where I grew up. My mother, Louisa S. Robinson, was head librarian at Claflin for decades; my father taught at the school for a time. . . . It was obvious that my life was different from the lives of the kids growing up in Sunnyside, a neighborhood of shotgun shacks where abject poverty and noxious dysfunction were evident for all to see. But it was a given that the factors that might have divided us were far outweighed by a single attribute that both defined and united us: We were all black, and to be black was to live under assault. That was just the way things were. It didn't matter how well you might have been dressed or how many college degrees you might have had. If a restaurant didn't offer service to "colored" people, you weren't going to eat there. If the city built a new whites-only playground, you kept out. If a redneck in a pickup truck wanted to yell "Nigger!" at the first black person he saw, you were eligible.

"I don't want to give the wrong impression. I think of my childhood as idyllic, and it never would have occurred to either my sister, Ellen, or me to entertain the notion that the South's system of white hegemony had anything to do with intelligence, ability, or merit. If anything, our environment suggested the opposite: The black Orangeburg we knew was cultured, well-traveled, and urbane, while the white Orangeburg we saw around us—basically a commercial depot and service center for an agricultural belt—seemed unlettered and uncouth. When I . . . went to the newly integrated Orangeburg High, which previously had been the whites-only high school in town—I learned that some white people were better than I had thought and some were worse. . . ."

So we were deep into Jim Crow, into a pervasive and sometimes vicious discrimination on the basis of race that, of course, extended to politics and voting as well. Jim Crow was a system profoundly unjust and beset by internal contradiction, but as a young boy it seemed settled as "a way of life." I did not hear much by way of defense of this system growing up, and certainly not much by way of dissent or criticism of it from the white community. The school desegregation case, *Brown v. Board of Education*, came down in 1954, when I was twelve, and when I graduated six years later from OHS, the entire school system was still 100 percent segregated, as was everything else. Things were stirring in the 1950s. The civil rights revolution was gathering strength, especially in the years after *Brown*. One of the *Brown* cases challenging segregation was from Clarendon County, bordering Orangeburg County, and the local minister who spearheaded the litigation, The Reverend J. A. DeLaine, had his home and church burned down in 1955. The murder of Emmett Till, the courageous act of Rosa Parks, the emergence of Martin Luther King Jr., the start of the white citizens' councils, South Carolina Senator Strom Thurmond's record-breaking filibuster of the 1957 civil rights legislation, President Eisenhower's decision to send federal troops to Little Rock to enforce a court's desegregation order and more all happened after *Brown*, as we the white kids at OHS carried on as if the outside world did not exist.

I did absorb by osmosis, by being part of the culture, the argument for segregation—the roots of the community's prejudice and mine. The year Cameron and I graduated from

OHS, 1960, also saw the publication of W. D. Workman's *The Case for the South*.[2] Workman, a fellow South Carolinian, was a substantial citizen and journalist. Later he became editor of the state's leading newspaper, *The State*, and ran as an early South Carolina Republican for the US Senate. His *The Case for the South* is an accurate, if painful, statement of the views widely held by white middle-class residents of South Carolina during my youth. In other words, these are the views I was brought up to believe, and did, Lord forgive me.

It was common for white Southerners to feel under attack from the North or, indeed, the rest of the country. And that is how Workman began: "The South is being scourged by four pestilential forces which impose an almost intolerable burden upon Americans who cherish state sovereignty, constitutional government, and racial integrity. On the one hand are these three: the Supreme Court of the United States, which has wrought havoc in its injudicious effort to play at sociology; the National Association for the Advancement of Colored People, which has recklessly undertaken to achieve race-mixing by pressure; and the Northern politicians and propagandists who pervert small truths into big lies as they purvey vilification and ignorance on a grand scale. On the other hand is the Ku Klux Klan with its unlovely cohorts who substitute muscle and meanness for the intellect which by rights must be the defense of the South."

Workman devoted much of the book to a critique of the *Brown v. Board of Education* decision and to defending "states' rights" and the Southern way of life apart from segregation. His case for continuing segregated schools and Jim Crow included a discussion of how black people and white people differed, and Workman set out views on racial inferiority I often heard growing up: "It is meaningless to tell a white Southerner that a Negro has the same hopes and capabilities of the white man, for even a cursory glance at any meter of morality shows that the two races are separated into opposing camps. . . . The white Southerner . . . refuses to accept any commingling of his children with the black children who have been raised in such an amoral culture. . . . There is a story illustrative of the point: The white man boss who professes wonderment at the capacity of his Negro employee to raise so much unmitigated hell every week-end hears this explanation: 'Boss, if you could be a nigger for jes' one Satiddy night, you'd never want to be a white man ag'in!' That story portrays the 'earthiness' of the Negro character, the preference for living in the flesh rather than in the mind."

It is worth taking some time, here, with Workman's book, because it is important to understand the mind of the white South. After recounting statistics comparing blacks and whites in communicable diseases, illegitimacy, promiscuity, and delinquency, he returns to the theme of racial integrity: "Perhaps even more basically, there is the additional fear that impure blood will supplant the pure over a period of time, leading to an inevitable and ultimate corruption of all. . . . Bit by bit, the grand strategy of the integration plan is making itself discernible. . . . And it must follow, as the night the day, that the next goal is amalgamation, hybridization, or mongrelization, depending upon how plain or fancy one wishes to be in describing the same thing. . . .

"There is a fierce pride of race among Southerners . . . and that pride countenances no adulteration of the white family stock. . . . If intermarriage on a considerable scale were to result, there could be no effective turning back by the time the mistake were discovered. Racial admixture, or 'mongrelization' as it is denominated in the South, has a snow-balling effect. Once started, it grows of its own momentum and resistance to its acceleration becomes harder and harder. The same analogy pertains to the moral involvements, for there would result inevitably a relaxing of moral objections to hybridization, once hybrids themselves were present in appreciable numbers among the policy-setting social group."

Workman continues, "Perhaps more than any other single factor, this apprehension [of interracial sexual relations] has solidified white resistance to integration." Then he adds: "The impulse toward sexual gratification on the part of Negro men generally is a matter of common knowledge among both races in the South, and seems to be accepted by both—with this par-amount qualification: Negro men must never cross the color line. The fear of swift, certain and severe punishment hangs sword-like over the head of the Southern Negro who entertains thoughts of consorting with a white woman, and white South-erners firmly believe that in the absence of that deterrent fear, there would be no restraining of Negro men."

Well, there we have it: a voice from a half-century ago, disgusting views, but an accurate summation of the dominant white thinking of 1960. Never mind that Strom Thurmond had decades earlier fathered a mixed-race child. Never mind that many of the smartest, best-educated, and hardest-working citizens of Orangeburg were black faculty and staff members at South Carolina State and Claflin and that many of them were products of what Workman called "mongrelization," which stretches back to the days before the founding of the republic. And now one of Workman's so-called "hybrids" is president of the United States. The world has indeed changed, thanks largely to the civil rights activists who put it all on the line and often paid dearly for it. But the legacy of the racism reflected in Workman's book is still a powerful force in America.

Of course there were other, different white voices in the South at this time. Notable among them was James McBride Dabbs. Dabbs grew up on his family's antebellum plantation, Rip Raps, near Mayesville, South Carolina, in Sumter County, very close to Orangeburg. He became chair of the English department at Coker College in Hartsville, South Carolina, at the time Cameron's mother Ethel was a student there. The rise of the civil rights concern in the 1940s and 1950s led him to think through the issue, and by 1957 he was president of the Southern Regional Council. Headquartered in Atlanta, it was a powerful voice for racial justice and equality.

In 1958, two years before Workman's book, Dabbs had published *The Southern Heritage*.[3] It took a stand firmly against segregation. He praised "the Southern way of life"—love of the land and tradition, a sense of place and family, leisure, and good manners—but saw segregation as something "in sharp contrast to the rest of Southern life." Regarding whites' treatment of blacks, "We were wrong much of the time, and much of the time we knew it." And at the end of his great book, he wrote: "Through the processes of history and the grace of God we have been made one people, and . . . it is disastrous to talk and act as if we were two. If, on the contrary, we would play the game wholeheartedly together, if we would be our deepest selves, there is no telling what great age might develop in the South. . . . The white Southerner is the man he is because he has lived among Negroes, and they are the people they are because they have lived with him. We don't have to do anything about it; we have only to accept the fact. The basic fact of our lives. . . .

If Southerners could rise to the level of loving passionately, not only their hills and valleys, as they do, but also the rich and varied configuration of people, black and white, who dwell therein, with the untold possibilities for achievement which lie in such association, we should not only solve our greatest problem, one of the two major problems of the world today, but our age would become a challenge to generations as yet unborn. . . . Let us accept now such a challenge as will astonish the world."

Dabbs was articulating the myth or dream of the biracial South, the idea that in the South, because blacks and whites had lived together so closely, they could now build a racially harmonious society and live together in mutual respect. Progressive whites would repeat the dream often in the decades to come, and it is there, plain as day, in the speeches of Martin Luther King Jr. and other black leaders.

The year his book came out, Dabbs was interviewed for television by a young Mike Wallace.[4] Wallace asked Dabbs, "Can an average Southerner ever totally free himself from his emotional feeling about the Negro simply by telling himself or having our Supreme Court telling him that segregation is wrong?" Dabbs's answer was profound: "No, you can't reason about the thing. Most Southerners won't reason about it at all. The only change, the only way I see for this fundamental psychological change to occur, is for the South to get new pictures and new images of what it wants, for instance a new picture of the Negro." And Dabbs came out powerfully for federal actions to push a recalcitrant white South: "The South may still hope that the union, the nation, now will back down and leave the South to do what it wishes. The nation can't back down. . . . It's the key issue, our relation to the colored peoples of the world. . . .

It's more fundamental than communism and democracy. . . This is a bigger issue. This issue will be disturbing the world longer than the democratic–communistic issue. Now the nation cannot withdraw and let the South do what it wishes."

I never heard of Dabbs until I was at Yale.

I arrived at Yale in the fall of 1960, just as the civil rights movement was gathering the strength that would make all the difference. My initial and all-consuming focus, though, was doing well in my courses. For the first time in my life, I felt challenged academically. In that regard, some interesting and very positive things happened freshman year. Connecticut Hall, Yale's oldest building, is close to my old room in Vanderbilt Hall, and it was my favorite place to study. One evening quite late I was folding up my chemistry book and materials and heading back to Vanderbilt when a fellow sufferer said to me, "Have you got that Bohr atom stuff under control?" I was startled. "What Bohr atom stuff?" "Here," he said, "you better go over this. It might be on the exam tomorrow." And he handed me a batch of mimeographed handouts from the class, a session I must have slept through. And, of course, the Bohr atom was the centerpiece of the exam, which I aced, so much so that the chair of the chemistry department would later write my parents a letter about my high final grade in chemistry. Consider the alternative!

My freshman English course was taught by a woman professor named Bernhard in a classroom above Phelps Gate. We were required to produce a serious paper for her, and I wrote mine on "The Use of Vegetation in 'Death in Venice.'" Why I chose that topic, I have no idea, but once you focus on it, Thomas Mann's use of natural settings, gardens, fruit, and images of nature is fascinating. Shortly after handing in my paper, Bernhard called me to her office, a small room in the basement of Harkness Hall, and she said to me, "Is this original?" I replied that it was, hoping that she would believe me and that would be the end of it. And then she said, "I have to be sure before I submit it for a freshman writing prize." I was shocked and shocked again later when I was awarded the prize.

We are carried forward by others. These were affirming events for someone from Orangeburg High struggling to do well at Yale. At some level, I must have said to myself, "I can do this thing."

But something else happened to me early on, again in Connecticut Hall. I was studying in one of the seminar rooms there when someone I did not know stuck his head in the door and said in a library voice, "Can we talk to you?" I followed him into the hall, whereupon he and another white upperclassman grabbed me with some violence and slammed me hard against the wall and angrily growled, "If you ever say 'nigger' or any other racist shit, we will beat you to a pulp, understand?" I have no recollection of having said or done anything to provoke this attack, but somehow they had identified me as a Southern boy who might.

Angels do not always seem like angels. These guys offended and disturbed me, but they and others forced me to think hard. The early 1960s were years of major escalation in the civil rights movement—the sit-ins began in 1960, the Student Nonviolent Coordinating Committee (SNCC) was established that year, and the Congress of Racial Equality (CORE) launched freedom rides in 1961. John Lewis and others, black and white, were beaten by a mob in Montgomery. In Orangeburg in 1963 hundreds of black demonstrators, mostly students, were assaulted with water hoses and tear gas and arrested. Bless them, many Yale students took up the fight for racial equality. Indeed, thanks to our chaplain William Sloane Coffin in particular, Yale was a leader in student activism in support of civil rights. At Yale, I was frequently challenged personally on my views, and often I felt that my family and friends back home and, indeed, the South generally were under attack, vilified, dismissed as bigots who had to be pushed aside.

Looking back, I can see that, prompted by all this, three personal "projects" took shape, and after freshman year I pursued them with some determination while in school: an effort to free myself from the curse of the bigotry I had learned; an effort to convince anyone who would listen that preserving truly valuable parts of the Southern heritage required a different approach to ending Jim Crow; and an effort to convince my adult friends back home in Orangeburg that they should get moving with desegregation and new opportunities for blacks before it was too late.

First, I set about to truly understand the South and, relatedly, to move beyond the prejudice and provincialism I had absorbed in Orangeburg. Through the end of sophomore year I was a biochemistry major, and I have never regretted the heavy dose of science I got in those years. But when I was told by my faculty advisor what I should take my remaining two years, including tons more science and even German, I jumped ship, into political science. Thereafter, any time I could focus a term paper on the South—its history, its economics, its politics, its impact on US foreign affairs—I did. My best effort, I think, was "Republicanism and Realignment in South Carolina: 1948–1960," which traced the rise of the Republican Party in the state and showed how powerfully its origins were rooted in the Dixiecrat movement led by Strom Thurmond in 1948, when he and others broke away from the Democratic party to promote states' rights and segregation. The official Dixiecrat party was short-lived, but those who bolted the Democratic fold that year never came back in national elections. When I worked for *The State* newspaper in 1964, in the midst of the Republican and Democratic conventions, I wrote two long articles for the paper based on this analysis.

A book I turned to early on was W. J. Cash's *The Mind of the South* (1941). It had a powerful influence on me. Cash found both positives and negatives about the South and sought to disentangle the positives from the worst of the negatives: the shame of racism and segregation.[5] I will never forget how Cash summed up his view of the white Southerner: "Proud, brave, honorable by its lights, courteous, personally generous, loyal, swift to act, often too swift, but signally effective, sometimes terrible, in its action—such was the South at its best. And such at its best it remains today, despite the great falling away in some of its virtues. Violence, intolerance, aversion and suspicion toward new ideas, an incapacity for analysis, an inclination to act from feeling rather than from thought, an exaggerated individualism and a too narrow concept of social responsibility, attachment to fictions and false values, above all too great attachment to racial values and a tendency to justify cruelty and injustice in the name of those values, sentimentality and a lack of realism—these have been its characteristic vices in the past. And, despite changes for the better, they remain its characteristic vices today."

The Mind of the South helped me sort things out, and I recall referring to it in my interview for a Rhodes Scholarship in 1964. Whatever I said must have made some sense. It helped also to have good friends at Yale with whom I could discuss things, and my fellow students Charles Post and Wallace Winter were that for me.

This digging, and hoping that by understanding I could exorcise my demons, continued through senior year when, in lieu of regular courses, three distinguished Yale professors—a sociologist, a political scientist, and an historian—each agreed to special one-on-one tutorials with me on various aspects of Southern life, culture, and history, and the dean of American political science, Robert Dahl, allowed me to take his graduate seminar.

The historian who had generously agreed to spend an hour or so each week was none other than C. Vann Woodward, whose *The Strange Career of Jim Crow* had been enormously influential for me. At some point in the semester, Woodward asked me my personal view on ongoing events in the South and in Orangeburg in particular where earlier, in the fall of 1963, over 1,000 civil rights protestors had been arrested. I followed up my answer with a note to him that in part said, "The real question facing the South today is how to die. We can take our sentiments and prejudices and bury them somewhere deep inside us and get about the pressing task of coming to grips with the problems of our century. Or we can commit suicide, as Orangeburg is doing now—killing its spirit to save its honor and ending in foolishness."

Sophomore year I rushed St. Anthony Hall, a combination fraternity and secret society. It was one of my best decisions at Yale; I found most of my closest friends at Yale there. As we prospective pledges were each being quizzed by existing members—why do you want to join St. Anthony Hall?—I was asked if I would object to having a black member of the Hall. I said no, not at all, and thought to myself, maybe they are testing me. It turns out that they were asking all of us that question, and not as a test. It was real. They had decided to admit a black student. That night my good friend Wendell Motley became the first black member of St. Anthony Hall. Wendell would go on to sprint for Trinidad in the Olympics and later become that country's finance minister. In response, the national fraternity promptly suspended the Yale chapter. Those guys had not only integrated the Hall at Yale, they had integrated the whole national frat. That's how it was in 1961, and apparently it is still that way in places judging from the 2013 announcement that Alabama was moving to integrate sororities in the state! After a while, the suspension was lifted.

The second project I took up at Yale was something of a rear-guard action—trying to convince any of my fellow Yalies who would listen that most Southern whites were good people and not full of racial hatred, that there were many admirable characteristics of the South that care should be taken to preserve, and that efforts to achieve racial equality in the South, instead of confrontation, should focus on creating an environment that allowed Southerners to step up and address their own problem. I soon, but not soon enough, came to see this approach as embarrassingly naïve. For most of my time at Yale, I was carrying a torch for the South.

Sometime late in my Yale undergraduate years, I decided I should try to do something about the problems I kept talking about. So I dropped the idea of becoming a doctor, where I had retreated after dropping the scientist idea, and I decided instead to return to South Carolina for a life in public affairs, thinking I might go into politics. That meant law school, not med school. I have the notes I used to prepare my application to Yale Law School during senior year, and they say: "The South today is faced with a large number of problems which must be solved in the near future. An unbalanced economy, a dearth of capable political leadership, severely limited opportunities for Negro citizens—these are a few of the more pressing. As a Southerner, I am interested in seeing these problems solved by the people who must live with the solutions and in a manner which preserves what is truly valuable in the South. . . . My plans include returning to South Carolina and exerting whatever positive leadership I am capable of on the future social and economic development of the South. Since the problems of the area and their solutions all have legal aspects and ramifications, a rigorous training in law is an ideal preparation."

This new idea of what to do with myself would continue as my guiding star for several years. In fact, I planned to go into politics up until my unsettling experience as Eugene McCarthy's campaign coordinator in South Carolina during the summer of 1968 after my second year at law school. I had taken up the antiwar cause, and my job was to try to get South Carolina votes for Clean Gene—running on a promise for a speedy withdrawal of troops from Vietnam—at the Chicago convention. The convention was a gas, figuratively and literally. I can still smell the tear gas Mayor Daley's police used to disperse us. But, try as I might, I ended up with only one vote for McCarthy. One. All the others supported the state Democratic leadership's goal of delivering the full delegation for Hubert Humphrey. Though my efforts were hardly successful, it was a delightful irony of history for the South Carolina governor, Robert McNair, and other state Democratic leaders to side with Humphrey, the man who had so inflamed the South in his pro-civil rights speech at the 1948 convention that Strom Thurmond and others fled the party and became Dixiecrats. In the end, Richard Nixon carried South Carolina and, of course, the country.

I learned that summer what played well in South Carolina politics and what didn't, what was plausible and what wasn't, and I realized that my views had become detached from my Carolina roots and drifted too far to the left to allow a political career in the state. Thus ended my short career in Southern politics. That was a blessing in disguise, truly. South Carolina politics are much farther to the right today than in 1968. Fritz Hollings, a progressive Governor and US Senator, is ninety-two as I write. I wish he were thirty again. He is the kind of enlightened leader the state now needs so badly.

I have always been happy that one of my fellow South Carolinians at Yale Law School made a decision quite different from mine. John Spratt and I became friends when we were at Oxford together. John did return to South Carolina after law school, served his community, York and Rock Hill, for over a dozen years, and then just when I thought he might be settling into the quiet life of upstate South Carolina, he ran for the US Congress and won. John served in Congress for twenty-eight years, until 2011. He was a progressive Democrat and became chair of the House Budget Committee. There are many who say he was the most widely respected member of the House of Representatives.

My conflicted situation regarding civil rights surfaced in a memorable event in my life when Martin Luther King Jr. came to Yale for the 1964 graduation to receive his then controversial honorary doctoral degree. King had been bailed out of jail in St. Augustine so he could arrive at Yale, and the Charleston *News and Courier*, editorializing on Yale's decision, said that "Doctor of Terror" would be a fitting title for his degree. At one point in the ceremonies, as I was seated with my parents, King came walking by. People sprang to their feet in a standing ovation, but Daddy stayed sternly seated, and Mom followed suit. I remember being torn, not in my own views—by then King was my hero, too—but mainly not wanting to embarrass or hurt my parents. I recall that after a moment or two, I stood up and joined in the applause.

It was painful to conclude, as I had done at Yale, that I, my family, and my community had accepted and perpetuated a monstrous injustice toward African Americans and that the great bulk of what I had come to believe was nonsense or worse. Yet, when one's worldview and the institutions one believes in collapse, it can be, I found, entirely liberating. I was, it dawned on me, free to see things anew, to form my own views about what was important, and to develop a fresh take on the world unencumbered by any cultural or family inheritance. It was not wise, I had learned, to uncritically accept the status quo. This unmooring, breaking free of the past, was the first big step along a path that would lead me far away from my conservative Southern roots to a place that no longer fits comfortably on the spectrum of mainstream American politics. I realized about this time that I had, thank goodness, sidled away from the wrong side of history and that I never wanted to get close to it again. I had accepted one grave injustice, and I was determined not to let that happen a second time.

These were the seeds that sprouted in my later work for the environment, and, eventually, also for economic and system change. But as I look back over the years of higher education, there is one cause that is largely and painfully absent—the cause of civil rights. Oh, I became a supporter all right, but I never threw myself wholly into the movement. I wasn't sleepwalking through history, but I was mostly on the sidelines. I have always regretted that. The main place I did try to make a contribution to civil rights was in Orangeburg. That story I'll take up next.

THREE

Orangeburg 1968

*1*968 was a fateful year. Martin Luther King Jr. was murdered in April that year, as was Robert Kennedy two months later. In *1968: The Year That Rocked the World*, Mark Kurlansky writes about that contradictory, conflict-filled moment: "The year 1968 was a terrible year and yet one for which many people feel nostalgia. Despite the thousands dead in Vietnam [and] the murder of the two Americans who most offered the world hope, to many it was a year of great possibilities and is missed. . . . The thrilling thing about the year 1968 was that it was a time when significant segments of population all over the globe refused to be silent about the many things that were wrong with the world. They could not be silenced. There were too many of them, and if they were given no other opportunity, they would stand in the street and shout about them. And this gave the world a sense of hope that it has rarely had, a sense that where there is wrong, there are always people who will expose it and try to change it."[1]

1968 was also a difficult year of reckoning for Orangeburg. Two months before King's shooting, three young black students, protesting for equal rights as so many others had, were shot dead in Orangeburg by state highway patrol officers. In what has come to be known as the Orangeburg Massacre, at least twenty-eight others were wounded when the officers opened fire into the demonstrators on the campus of South Carolina State. The black community in Orangeburg, especially the students, had refused to be silenced; they shouted their grievances more loudly than ever before. And then the guns went off. It took three decades for the state of South Carolina and Orangeburg's white community to begin to come to terms with what happened that February. Even today the issue divides Orangeburg. The black community hopes for justice too long delayed, and many whites are still in denial, while some simply refuse to talk about the matter.

The tragedy is compounded by the fact that throughout the 1960s opportunities arose for Orangeburg to set itself on the road to racial progress. Good people, black and white, created those opportunities, but they were missed, not seized. Had they been, the Orangeburg Massacre might not have happened. We will never know.

I was involved in a modest way in encouraging such opportunities, and I will tell that story, helped by two remarkable observers. Jack Bass is one of our country's top journalists. He grew up in Orangeburg County about twenty miles up the Edisto River in the town of North. I became friends with him when I worked for *The State* newspaper in 1964 and he was already an established and well-regarded reporter. Bass would go on to become a Nieman Fellow at Harvard, a top recognition for journalists, and to write several award-winning books

about Southern politics and race relations. When the Orange-
burg tragedy occurred in early February 1968, he was South
Carolina bureau chief for the *Charlotte Observer*, and he and *Los
Angeles Times* star reporter Jack Nelson covered those events.
They went on to coauthor the book, *The Orangeburg Massacre*.
More than anything else, their book has forced those events,
and what really happened, into public consciousness.

More recently, a young professor at Denison University, Jack
Shuler, has written another profound book about the massacre
and its aftermath, *Blood and Bone: Truth and Reconciliation in a
Southern Town*. Shuler, it turns out, grew up in Orangeburg and
is the son of a high school friend of mine who lived not far from
us on Middleton Street.

Orangeburg was the scene of at least three major incidents
during the civil rights movement. The first occurred early
on, in the wake of the *Brown v. Board of Education* decision. In
1955, shortly after that decision, the Orangeburg branch of
the NAACP petitioned for immediate integration of the town's
public schools. In their book *The Palmetto State*, Bass and his
coauthor Scott Poole relate how that petition prompted a
well-organized response from the white community. Quickly,
citizens' councils, made up essentially of middle-class whites,
rose up in Orangeburg County to mobilize public opinion
against integration. Indeed, Orangeburg County was the center
of the white citizens' council movement in the state.

The Orangeburg white citizens' council, write Bass and
Poole, "played on fears of miscegenation, attacked organized
labor, and launched a campaign of economic reprisal. The
campaign targeted the signers of the integration petition. . . .
Those employed by whites who refused to withdraw their
names from the petition were fired. Many blacks lost their

jobs, local banks called in loans, some retailers refused to sell to black customers, and milk firms stopped deliveries to homes of signers."[2] In response, the local NAACP organized a highly effective counter-boycott against local businesses, and within a few weeks the council's campaign collapsed.

Bass and Poole observe that, "With its defeat in Orangeburg, citizens' councils saw membership dwindle from a statewide peak of forty thousand in the summer of 1956 to less than a thousand by 1963. The council activity in Orangeburg and elsewhere had served as a catharsis that absorbed the emotional fervor, and the state entered a temporary period of massive resistance.... As the civil rights movement expanded throughout the South and exploded in violence in Alabama, Mississippi, and elsewhere, South Carolina received little national attention."

I was in junior high when these events occurred, and looking back, I am surprised how little we young white kids focused on them. I guess the town's adults knew the civil rights movement would hit home eventually, but until that time they were happy to go whistling Dixie past the graveyard. They certainly did not discuss the matter around young people. Some may have thought Orangeburg could stay above the fray, or at least out of it.

Once in the early 1960s, when I was home from Yale, I went to visit with Benner Turner, a Harvard graduate who was then president of South Carolina State, which was then entirely black. He was pleased to discuss race issues with me, and was very cordial. I asked Dr. Turner, "Why are things peaceful here, but exploding in Alabama, Arkansas, and Mississippi?" To which he replied, "Well, Gus, I think we have a better class of people up here in South Carolina." I was stunned. A leading black citizen of Orangeburg had just said something that I could have heard from a bridge club friend of my mother. Was Dr. Turner sincere, or was he, like Dr. Bledsoe, the black college president in Ralph Ellison's *Invisible Man*, superbly adept at currying white favor? I have never been sure but I suspect some of both. Turner was not favorable toward the NAACP and was viewed negatively by the civil rights advocates in Orangeburg. In any case, as we shall see, Orangeburg would not stay peaceful for long.

While at Yale, I began to do what I could to encourage the moderates in Orangeburg to lead an effort to accept desegregation and deal with the deplorable conditions that racial injustice had brought about. So I began to write letters and make calls. One such letter was to my Granddaddy's good friend, Rut Osborne, who for many years was chair of the board of the University of South Carolina. "I guess what I'm saying," I wrote Mr. Rut in 1962, "is that it is my opinion, for what it's worth, that we in the South (in South Carolina, in Orangeburg) should begin now to voluntarily desegregate. . . . We have much to gain by this (the preservation of our self-respect and honor) and nothing to lose (for its going to be forced on us no matter what we do)."

Another truly fine person with whom I was in contact was Bill Clark, my former football coach who was then the principal of a junior high in Orangeburg. His handwritten reply to me is postmarked August 10, 1963, just before the March on Washington for Jobs and Freedom.

Dear Gus:

Received your kind letter and as I have a few moments will try and bring you up to date. Everything is touch and go at the present moment but I am optimistic that we may take a short step in the right direction in a few days.

Our meeting was held with about ten persons in attendance . . . The consensus was that we should establish communications with the Negro leaders. . . . We met with the mayor and it was quite an enlightening session. . . . It appears to me that somehow or other he just hopes the problem will go away. We finally extracted his head from the sand and he promised that he would appoint a committee if we would find reputable people to serve. Tommy [Tisdale, see below] and I then prepared a statement that we felt individuals and/or business firms could sign without committing themselves to any specific desegregation steps at the present moment. It says essentially that business firms and individuals "pledge to support the efforts of the Mayor's Community Relations Committee to sustain good will . . . etc. etc." We feel that if we can get a majority of the businesses and some of our leading citizens to endorse such a statement, we will be successful in finding persons to serve on the committee. We then plan to run a full page ad in the newspaper, with the pledge of support, the signatures, and at the same time an announcement of formation of the committee by the mayor. . . .

The time has been reached when we need some of our leaders in the community to take a stand. And in this I have been most disappointed. . . .

Best regards,
Bill Clark

Clark would remain disappointed. Little came of the effort he describes. Meanwhile, that summer and on into the fall of 1963, South Carolina's black leaders were pushing city by city across the state for equal access to public facilities and other reforms. Orangeburg's response—determined opposition—attracted national attention. The *New York Times* reported on October 20, 1963, "A new spirit in South Carolina calls for white leaders to make minimum concessions to Negro civil rights demands if necessary to preserve peace and prosperity. Orangeburg, however, has not got the message."[3]

Orangeburg's failure to concede anything to the black community's list of ten objectives led to massive demonstrations in mid-October and the arrest of 1,300 student protesters from South Carolina State, Claflin, and all-black Wilkinson High. The *New York Times* story reported that in Orangeburg "Negro and white communities here are as estranged as those in Alabama and Mississippi. Both sides see no sign of a reconciliation."

Reverend Tisdale, rector of the church my family attended and, like Bill Clark, a hero of mine then and still, brought me up to date in a letter he wrote me just a few days after these arrests:

Dear Gus,

It was good to talk with you. We need more concerned, interested and intelligent people like you in order to assert reason and work towards right and good solutions. Fixed prejudice and emotional frenzy are bad bedfellows. [Tisdale related a small bit of progress. The mayor had asked two representatives from the white community to meet with representatives of the black community. They had met once, and planned to do so again.]

It is little and late but perhaps better than nothing. There isn't much more that I can tell you until this group has an opportunity to reflect on the situation. There is quiet

now. It is either the calm before a worse storm or the begin-
ning of a new era for the community in which warmth and
good will may have a chance. It will be difficult either way.

With all good wishes, faithfully,
Thomas S. Tisdale

One can see in these fifty-year-old words of Clark and Tisdale both the struggle for hope and the shadow of its extinction.
They were fine, strong people of generous spirit and progressive
instinct. Two years after writing me, Clark would become
Orangeburg's superintendent of schools. Serving from 1965 to
1977, he presided over the desegregation of the town's public
schools. Tisdale actually had two congregations. In addition to
the all-white Church of the Redeemer, he was rector at a black
church near South Carolina State. But those were tense times,
and without support from the main civic leaders in town, there
was only so much they could do.

At some point later in my senior year at Yale, I received
a thirty-page document, unsigned and undated, but authored
by the Orangeburg moderates who were trying to get the town
moving in a constructive direction. The document, titled "The
Public Interest and the Future of Orangeburg as a Community," called for a series of citizen committees to be "established
under the overall co-ordination of the city administration to
study and make recommendations about various areas of our
present community problems."

The Orangeburg moderates prefaced their proposals with
an observation of what they were up against: "It is realized
that the mayor has stated publicly that there have not been
enough citizens willing to participate on even one community

committee and that a proposal for a series of them faces an even tougher prospect. However, it is believed that one of the major reasons volunteers have not been forthcoming is that one committee is expected to handle all of [the] complex and emotion-charged problems facing the city and as such it could be expected to become the focus of all the conflicting pressures in the community."

The authors proposed six committees in all: an Urban Redevelopment Committee to formulate a plan for the future development of the town with a focus on new low-rent housing; a Survey Committee to gather information on social and educational conditions and occupational skills and needs; an Employment Committee to address workplace bias with fair and objective qualifications and to promote wider employment opportunities; an Education Committee to study "the possibility of starting new programs within the school curriculum to which students of outstanding achievement would be admitted" as well as assigning students to schools "based on place of residence"; a Public Facilities Committee to address the problem of equal access to restaurants and other facilities; and, finally, an Interfaith Committee described as follows: "One such means of an expression of Christian values by the people of Orangeburg would be an Easter Sunday sunrise service held at the fairground stadium with participation by all our city's church groups. This would give us a chance to prove to ourselves that these values do have an applicability to our present human problems and that a common reaffirmation of them will be our best guide in what [at] moments may appear an insoluble predicament."

The authors of the document did not offer a full embrace of school or social integration, though they did mention assigning students to schools based on "place of residence." Black and white neighborhoods were cheek to jowl throughout Orangeburg. Yet, what a difference their recommendations could have made had they been earnestly pursued! And these voices of moderation understood well what was at stake: "More important than this growing isolation of groups and fragmentation of the community has been the question of human dignity. This value has been one of the most fundamental tenets of Southern Civilization and belief in it has brought the strength with which the South has withstood numerous tragedies. Now we are dangerously close to losing this value because there is a readiness to dispense with the love and respect that go with a recognition of the dignity of the human being rather than go through the difficult process of determining how recently achieved personal growth can be accorded recognition. When the dignity of any one individual is not given recognition, then the dignity of us all is diminished.

"If we begin to lose our sense of values then we lose the most important thing we have: A sense of community in which these values can be realized and in which meaning can be given to our lives. Without a sense of community our efforts to grow in wealth and wisdom must be in isolation without benefit of the growth of our fellows and without the satisfaction of contributing to others growth. The question that faces us is then whether we are prepared to lose what has been most valuable and distinctive about our life because we are not ready to handle the problems of the growth which this life has made possible."

The strained rationale for change—"recently achieved personal growth" in the black community—was how the town's moderates sought to explain their proposals to a white community drenched in a segregationist past. Unfortunately, even that did not work.

After graduating from Yale in 1964, I was able to land a summer job as a cub reporter for *The State* newspaper in Columbia. I lived at home in Orangeburg, and there I soon discovered that rather than moving forward with the ideas in the report just discussed, some in the town were preparing a giant step backward. In late June 1964 the Committee Investigating the Establishment of Private Schools, led by an old family friend, Elliott Wannamaker, issued its report. The report made it clear that Wannamaker and his group were not just seeking to perpetuate racial segregation but were also prepared to gravely damage the public school system in the process. It played on some old themes and fears: "While the members of this study group would shrink from imposing their view upon others, it is their conviction that the separation of the races in education, in recreation, in living quarters, and in churches is in the best interest of both races and is essential to the preservation of racial integrity. This conviction is supported by the observation that where different races have been compelled to or have voluntarily intermingled in these areas of social contact, the dire consequence of amalgamation has been consistently and indelibly recorded in every period of history—ancient, modern, and current. Therefore, due to the irreversible nature and the inevitability of the result anticipated, it is the consensus of this group that separate private school facilities must be provided, or some other means devised, which will avoid the pernicious 'experiment' being foisted upon the people of this state and nation."

I concluded that it was time for me to stop covering watermelon and peach festivals and their associated beauty contests and do some serious reporting, so I began writing stories for

The State about the private school proposal: "Private or Public School?" "Ministers Oppose Use of Churches as School Rooms." "A Community Is Divided." "Private Schools Not Dead." Clearly, I was engaged in advocacy journalism, so much so that *The State* decided to assign an experienced reporter to the story— and send me back to the festivals. My getting local ministers, especially Bill Lancaster at the First Baptist Church, on record against the use of church facilities for the private schools was particularly upsetting to Wannamaker, and I believe he complained about me to *The State*.

Despite considerable local opposition, Wannamaker and his supporters proceeded to establish the Wade Hampton Academy, one of the first of the hundreds of segregation academies to spread across the Deep South. It began operation in the fall of 1965. The South soon saw the birth of the Jefferson Davis Academy, the Stonewall Jackson Academy, the Robert E. Lee Academy, and even the Nathan Bedford Forrest Academy, named for the Confederate general who had helped to found the Klan and served as its first Grand Dragon. The sports teams at Wade Hampton were the Rebels.

The private school issue hit home. My sister Mary is seven years younger than I and was entering her junior year of high school when the Wade Hampton Academy opened. Cameron and I were on our honeymoon, but Mary reports that Daddy thought that she should go to the Academy, while Mom favored staying in OHS. Mom and Mary won that one, but that choice was not the usual one for white middle-class families in the area.

By 1971, when Orangeburg's public schools were integrated by court order, the two local "seg academies," as they are referred to by many, had 1,500 white students. In 1986 the Orangeburg academies enrolled 1,700 white students, the largest enrollment ever in a South Carolina independent school. Enrollment is down from that peak, but today the Orangeburg area public schools are about 85 to 90 percent black, and the now-named Orangeburg Prep is about 95 percent white.

These academies contributed to the loss of public support for, and white involvement in, the region's public schools—a great tragedy. And, of course, they have helped to thwart desegregation. Continuing residential segregation and, starting in the 1980s, a shift in the Supreme Court away from compelling integration, have joined the segregation academies and multiple forms of resistance in leading to a situation where actual separation of the races in education today—de facto segregation—is distressingly similar to what it was in the 1960s. Only 23 percent of black students in the United States attended white-majority schools in 2011, the lowest number since 1968.

Finishing my brief stint as a reporter, I left in September of 1964 for school in England. Cameron and I were married the following summer, the first year in history that Rhodes Scholars at Oxford were allowed to be married. Soon thereafter, I was buried in the *Yale Law Journal* and other undertakings at the Yale Law School. Then, halfway through law school, in February of 1968, Orangeburg exploded. The definitive account of the incident is Bass and Nelson's highly regarded *The Orangeburg Massacre*, published two years later in 1970. In 2003, thirty-five years after the event, Bass summarized for his fellow Nieman awardees what happened in February, 1968, and reflected on the aftermath. It's a critical story, one that Bass has pursued relentlessly, and I will give him ample space to tell it:[4] "At 10:33 p.m. on the night of February 8, 1968, eight to 10 seconds of police gunfire left three young black men dying and 28 wounded on the campus of South Carolina State College in Orangeburg.

Exactly 33 years later, Governor Jim Hodges addressed an over-flow crowd there in the Martin Luther King, Jr. Auditorium and referred directly to the 'Orangeburg Massacre'—an identifying term for the event that itself had been controversial among South Carolinians. Governor Hodges called what happened 'a great tragedy for our state' and expressed 'deep regret.' . . .

"For the first time, survivors [of the shootings] were honored at this annual memorial service for the three students who died, Samuel Hammond, Delano Middleton, and Henry Smith. Their deaths, which happened more than two years before gunfire by national guardsman in Ohio killed four students at Kent State University, marked the first such tragedy on any American college campus.

"Unlike Kent State, the students killed at Orangeburg were black, and the shooting occurred at night, leaving no compelling TV images. What happened barely penetrated the nation's consciousness. . . .

"The shootings occurred two nights after an effort by students at the then almost all-black college to bowl at the city's only bowling alley. The owner refused. Tensions arose and violence erupted. When it ended, nine students and one city policeman received hospital treatment for injuries. Other students were treated at the college infirmary. College faculty and administrators at the scene witnessed at least two instances in which a female student was held by one officer and clubbed by another.

"After two days of escalating tension, a fire truck was called to douse a bonfire lit by students on a street in front of the campus. State troopers—all of them white, with little training in crowd control—moved to protect the firemen. As more than 100 students retreated inside the campus, a tossed banister rail struck one trooper in the face. He fell to the ground bleeding.

Five minutes later, almost 70 law enforcement officers lined the edge of the campus. They were armed with carbines, pistols and riot guns—short-barreled shotguns that by dictionary definition are used 'to disperse rioters rather than to inflict serious injury or death.' But theirs were loaded with lethal buckshot, which hunters use to kill deer. Each shell contained nine to 12 pellets the size of a .32 caliber pistol slug.

"As students began returning to the front to watch their bonfire go out, a patrolman suddenly squeezed several rounds from his carbine into the air—apparently intended as warning shots. As other officers began firing, students fled in panic or dived for cover, many getting shot in their backs and sides and even the soles of their feet. . . .

"At a noon press conference the next day in Columbia, South Carolina, Governor Robert E. McNair called it 'one of the saddest days in the history of South Carolina' and referred to 'this unfortunate incident.' He expressed concern that the state's 'reputation for racial harmony had been blemished.' Contrary to all evidence, McNair also said the shooting occurred off campus. He placed blame on 'black power advocates' and added other inaccurate embellishments.

"In federal court more than a year later, a jury took less than two hours to acquit nine troopers charged with imposing summary punishment without due process of law. . . .

"The Associated Press initially misreported the shooting as 'a heavy exchange of gunfire'—and didn't correct it. In the aftermath of major urban riots, the national media's interest in civil rights faded, and what happened on the campus at Orangeburg, where the victims were black, was out of tune with the times and not considered 'news.' Few questioned Governor McNair's misleading account. . . ."

Two black demonstrators killed in the Orangeburg Massacre lie on the ground near South Carolina State College. Following three days of protests, three were killed and twenty-eight were wounded.

Among the seriously wounded that day was Orangeburg itself. Bass and Nelson say in their 2002 afterword in *The Orangeburg Massacre*, the story "has yet to penetrate with depth into America's consciousness."[5] That's still true. But it certainly penetrated the minds of the citizens of Orangeburg, black and white, in many ways. At least the shootings forced the mayor and the city council to move to set up a biracial Human Relations Commission, twenty whites and twenty blacks. Unfortunately, after a short while, the group ran out of steam and didn't contribute much to racial reconciliation or progress.

Some whites in Orangeburg have come to terms with what happened almost a half century ago, but many still struggle with it and still others claim, erroneously, that the state highway patrol troopers were shot at by students or that the whole thing was caused by SNCC organizer Cleveland Sellers. (Sellers, the only person to go to jail for these events, was later pardoned by South Carolina and subsequently became president of the historically black Voorhees College.)

It's interesting to speculate on the national impact of the Orangeburg Massacre and Governor McNair's handling of it. Before the 1968 Massacre, McNair's stock as a progressive Southern governor was very high. He was chair of both the Southern Governors' Association and the National Democratic Governors Association. His prominence and political skill earned him a spot on the shortlist to become Hubert Humphrey's running mate in the 1968 presidential campaign. He was vetted for the Democratic vice presidential candidate position along with a very few others. McNair would have greatly strengthened the Democratic ticket in the South, but his mishandling of the events in Orangeburg put an end to his hopes for higher office. Humphrey chose Edmund Muskie instead. The Humphrey-Muskie ticket did poorly in the South, carrying only Texas. It is at least possible that the Orangeburg Massacre helped elect Richard Nixon in 1968.

In 2009 and 2010 Jack Shuler returned to his native Orangeburg to "see what had changed in Orangeburg" since 1968. The result of almost forty interviews is an impressive book, *Blood and Bone*. He found a town moving toward a broader, common understanding, but also one that is still divided. "Race relations in contemporary Orangeburg hinge on addressing this issue," he observes. "The event, and how people understand it, represents the stalemate. And yet it also represents the promise of reconciliation and change."[6]

A leading black woman in Orangeburg told Shuler that still "there's anger." She wants a state investigation, a truth commission like the one that Desmond Tutu led in South Africa, and sees it as an important step forward to closure. "I'm not even talking about compensation. What is a conversation going to do? It's going to get some of the hurt, the anger, the pain, out. People were treated in a way that's not right. Until we get some sort of recognition and validation of that, then there's going to be anger and things aren't going to change. It's not to blame anyone; it's to talk about it." Others fear the issues may be too remote to get to the truth of the many controversies still alive. Shuler believes that "a state-sanctioned investigation could open up a public conversation that has yet to happen and give South Carolina and Orangeburg a new redemptive story. It could also validate the claims of violence and the concerns the students had in 1968."

A local black minister told Shuler that Orangeburg was still permeated with a "spirit of division" growing out of the Orangeburg Massacre. Interracial conversations and other efforts at reconciliation have been attempted, but he believes few want to discuss the real issues: "racism and its stepchildren distrust, fear and anger."

But he and other ministers in Orangeburg, white and black, related to Shuler their sense that there was genuine hope, stemming in part from the town's 137 churches. Black and white pastors have been meeting and talking regularly and "trading pulpits all around the community." Well-produced public radio and film documentaries and even a play have broadened awareness and reached in a positive way many who were previously out of the conversation. Two South Carolina governors have expressed regret and, with an Orangeburg mayor, offered apologies for the tragedy. On the thirty-third anniversary of the Massacre a group of civic leaders, both black and white, took out a full-page ad in the local newspaper carrying an essay about community reconciliation. There's a palpable sense in Orangeburg that things are finally moving. In 2013, Orangeburg elected its first-ever black mayor.

In February 2014, Cameron and I attended the forty-sixth commemoration of the Orangeburg Massacre, again in the Martin Luther King Jr. Auditorium at South Carolina State. It was a poignant event, with a large turnout from the families of those shot that day. John Stroman, who as a student led the bowling alley protests, spoke with restraint, but forty-six years later it was easy to detect his underlying anger and frustration at what happened before, during, and after the shootings. It brought home to Cameron and me the accuracy of Shuler's depiction.

Shuler's conclusion is bracing: "The violence of February 8, 1968, created a fissure in the community of Orangeburg to the extent that the event itself cannot be named—shooting, massacre, incident, riot. Violence is discordant; it ruptures humanity and language literally and figuratively. What shall we call that night? How shall we remember it? Whatever it was, it deserves our solemn reverence and reflection and our modest attempts to transform it into something else, into a new story. . . . It's much easier to offer pat responses to past atrocities—'it's time to move on'; 'they need to get over it'; 'live and let live'—than to address the dirt. And some things cannot be moved on from so easily. Reconciliation for Orangeburg means taking seriously what happened that night in February 1968. (Reconciliation must always be a place-specific phenomenon—in Sharpeville or in

Selma—confronting the underlying causes of what happened in a particular place, with a particular history.) Reconciliation means recognizing the trauma that continues in the lives of some of the shooting victims and perpetrators. It also means taking seriously the underlying issue—racism.

"Orangeburg is a symptom for a larger problem, and it needs to be discussed frankly. The bedrock of our national history is as much wrack and ruin, chattel slavery and native genocide, as it is the heroes of '76 and Lincoln's benevolence. We have to look at this history closely. We have to ask why so many of our nation's schools and neighborhoods are so segregated. We have to ask why we are so obsessed with race. These are Orangeburg's issues, but they are also those of New York, Los Angeles, and Des Moines."

I can no longer feel the texture of daily life in Orangeburg. I am happy to have Jack Shuler for that. But the town lives on in memory and in my heart. It is there, in poet Richard Wilbur's words, "Where, before our eyes, all the living and the dead meet without surprise." What are the most important words one can say to others? I think they are these: I will remember you fondly, always. There are so many people from Orangeburg, past and present, to whom I'd like to say that.

Shuler is right to point us to national challenges, challenges to which, I fear, the South has contributed a great deal. Let me turn to that subject next.

FOUR

South and Nation

Our country's leading advocate for children, Marian Wright Edelman, was born into the black community of Bennettsville, South Carolina, just a few years before I came into the world. Bennettsville is in the Pee Dee region of the state, not next door to Orangeburg but not far away either. There are some parallels in our lives, though her accomplishments certainly exceed mine. We both found our causes early on. She became a civil rights activist in college in 1960. After Yale Law School, she went to Mississippi as a civil rights attorney, where among other things she met her husband-to-be, Peter Edelman, who was then working with Attorney General Robert Kennedy. Later, she would found the Children's Defense Fund.

What is striking to me is that well into her career Edelman concludes that while we, as a nation, have come far over the past decades, we have also lost something important along the way. Here is how she describes it in her memoir, *Lanterns*:[1]

"In many ways, the labyrinth of my life is leading back to where I began and to many of the lessons learned but too easily lost in the cacophony of noise and clutter and triviality and depersonalization afflicting so much of modern American life and culture. With others, I seek to reweave the frayed remnants of family, community, and spiritual values rent asunder in the name of progress. That much racial, social, and scientific progress has taken place over my lifetime is evident. Millions of Black children and poor children of all races have moved into the American mainstream and are better off materially. But something important has been lost as we have thrown away or traded so much of our Black spiritual heritage for a false sense of economic security and inclusion. We are at risk of letting our children drown in the bathwater of American materialism, greed, and violence. We must regain our moral bearings and roots and help America recover hers before millions more children—Black, Brown, and White, poor, middle-class, and rich—self-destruct or grow up thinking life is about acquiring rather than sharing, selfishness rather than sacrifice, and material rather than spiritual wealth."

Edelman is right, I think, that something important has been lost. As she says, we Americans have sacrificed much of our cultural, spiritual, and, I would add, environmental heritage to the god we call Progress. The values of caring for each other and for future generations, of community and solidarity, of reverence for life have been diminished in the relentless rise of materialism and consumerism and our fetishing of economic ends and means. That is the American tragedy, and it is at the root of so many of our gravest challenges as a society.

I will try here to tell the story of that loss from my perspective, as a white Southerner. It is a story that involves what happened to the South in my lifetime and also how the South has profoundly influenced the nation.

When the white South began to be seriously challenged for its Jim Crow ways, I and many others talked about the distinctive qualities of Southern life and culture, endangered qualities worth defending and saving even if segregation wasn't. At Yale, as I struggled with my Southern upbringing, I encountered many descriptions of the South's distinctiveness, some more generous than W. J. Cash's, which I quoted earlier. Here is one that resonated with me, from American studies professor Louis Rubin's take on the South, written in the late 1950s:[2]

"History and economic necessity forced certain virtues upon Southern life. Through no fault of its own, the South evolved a civilization that did not place its reliance upon the material goods of life, but upon the values of individuality, self-reliance, the community arts, a life which did not allow getting and spending to interfere with leisurely, relaxed living. The way of life which permitted a man to enjoy himself, to know the satisfaction of being something more than a cog in a machine—at its typical best this was the attainment of civilization in the South. At its heart was an historical sense of life, an instinctive realization that man was not a creature of chance and the moment. It was a life that emphasized the right relationship of man to nature and the essential dependence of man on nature. It was a life of the spirit as well as the flesh, which provided in its makeup for recognition of the values of the spirit. It was a life of stasis, of acceptance, not one of restlessness and doubt. This is the life that is threatened by the coming of industrialism to the South, and these are the values that the dominance of the industrial community most menaces."

Writing a little more than a decade later, journalist Jonathan Yardley would sum up the South's virtues in a similar way: "Love for and closeness to the land; a strong and intimate sense of family; an awareness of the past and its hard lessons; genuine hospitality, civility and courtliness; perhaps most of all, a sense of community."[3]

These descriptions, idealized for sure, fit rather well what I experienced in Orangeburg in the 1950s, as my story of growing up there reflects. But even as Rubin and Yardley wrote, things were changing. Rubin notes that many of the South's virtues were forced by "history and economic necessity." But after World War II, the South's burden of economic necessity began to lift. Choices opened up.

One possibility was the dream of the biracial South. If the white South could outgrow its racism, blacks and whites together could accomplish amazing things—the South could "astonish the world," Dabbs says. Charles Black, a Texan, was a leading constitutional law professor when I was at Yale Law. A decade earlier he had written that he had long had a dream, one for which there was no basis in history or sociology but one formed by his own experience, as a white man, with the many black Southerners he had known, "both in the North and at home." He noted "again and again how often we laugh at the same things, how often we pronounce the same words the same way to the amusement of our hearers, judge character in the same frame of reference, mist up at the same kinds of music. . . . My dream is simply that sight will one day clear and that each of the participants will recognize the other. If the two could join and look toward the future together—something would have happened uniquely beautiful in history. The South, which has always felt itself reserved for a high destiny, would have found it, and would come to flower at last."[4]

That was the dream. If the South could preserve the way of life described by Rubin and Yardley while transcending its racial prejudices and bigotry, then we would have something quite remarkable. I thought about and spoke often of that dream at Yale. Today, the dream of a biracial South is still alive to a limited degree. After the passage of the civil rights legislation of the 1960s, race relations in the South did improve. The Great Migration of blacks to the North reversed, and a million blacks have now returned to the South, mostly from the Northeast. Still, the South today is very far indeed from providing a model for the nation.

The dream of a distinctive, culturally attractive, biracial South was not to be. It's important to understand what happened instead. What we have seen in recent decades is not the preservation of the qualities described by Rubin and Yardley but the march of America's corporatist consumer society sweeping over the South, not merely unimpeded but warmly embraced. And, as I will discuss in a moment, these developments have been paralleled by the spread of some of the South's more deplorable attributes to the rest of America.

When I was at Yale, C. Vann Woodward pointed me to his essay "The Search for Southern Identity," first published in 1958.[5] Brilliant man that he was, he saw clearly what was happening: "The South is still in the midst of an economic and social revolution [that] has already leveled many of the old monuments of regional distinctiveness and may end eventually by erasing the very consciousness of a distinctive tradition along with the will to sustain it."

Woodward notes that the threat of being submerged under a national steamroller had long haunted the mind of the South and that some had sounded the alarm. "One of these entrenchments was that of the twelve Southerners who wrote *I'll Take My Stand*. They sought to define what they called 'a Southern way of life against what may be called the American or prevailing way,' and they agreed 'that the best terms in which to represent the distinction are contained in the phrase, Agrarian *versus* Industrial. . . .'

"Even in 1930 the agrarians were prepared to admit 'the melancholy fact that the South itself has wavered a little and shown signs of wanting to join up behind the common or American industrial ideal.' . . . Three decades later the slight 'wavering' in the Southern ranks that disturbed the agrarians in 1930 would seem to have become a pell-mell rout. . . . The voice of the South in the 1950s had become the voice of the chamber of commerce . . .

"The traditionalist who has watched the Bulldozer Revolution plow under cherished old values of individualism, localism, family, clan, and rural folk culture has felt helpless and frustrated against the mighty and imponderable agents of change. Industrialism, urbanism, unionism, and big government conferred or promised too many coveted benefits. They divided the people and won support in the south, so that it was impossible to rally unified opposition to them.

"The race issue was different. Advocates and agents of change could be denounced as outsiders, intruders, meddlers. Historic memories of resistance and cherished constitutional principles could be invoked. Racial prejudices, aggressions, and jealousies could be stirred to rally massive popular support. And with this dearly bought unity, which he could not rally on other issues, the frustrated traditionalist might at last take his stand for the defense of all the defiled, traduced, and neglected values of the traditional order."

In short, Woodward early on saw that what was called progress had begun to erase the cultural features of the South that many found attractive and that simultaneously the white South set about burnishing its worst racial instincts.

Woodward's metaphorical bulldozer continued to roll through the South in the fifty-five years since he wrote, my entire adult life. It can now be said of the contemporary South that it is like the rest of America, only more so. But that may be a case of seeing the matter backward, for a strange thing happened on the way to what was supposed to be the loss of Southern identity. Historian James Cobb, writing in 2005 in his book *Away Down South*, captured well what transpired:[6]

"*Saturday Review's* 1976 description of the South as 'the New America' had seemed to suggest not only that the region's long run as the nation's 'other' had finally come to an end but that a once ostracized Dixie might now actually show a stricken and uncertain nation how to rise above its divisions and doubts. Within a decade, however, many liberal observers were blaming the South's strong and still strengthening influence on national affairs for the emergence of what struck them as a very different 'New America,' this one rigidly conservative and at times even reactionary, its racism and intolerance, social indifference, and sometimes, its downright meanness, almost palpable."

Cobb observes that "the national embrace of so many of the activities and traits once deemed distinctly southern raises questions about how much longer they can be legitimately identified with the South."[7] John Egerton had warned in 1974, Cobb notes, "that neither the South nor the nation were benefiting from the 'Americanization of Dixie' or the 'Southernization of America' so much as they were simply 'sharing and spreading the worst in each other while the best languishes and withers.'"

The South has proven far more adept at exporting its vices than its virtues. A rancid politics combined with an ultraconservative social and economic agenda, an antipathy toward the federal government, an uncritical embrace of American exceptionalism, the rise of the religious right, racial prejudice and easy acceptance of de facto segregation—all reflect the influence of the South on national life.

Here is how *New York Times* reporter Peter Applebome describes the result in his 1997 book, *Dixie Rising*: "Think of a place that's bitterly antigovernment and fiercely individualistic, where race is a constant subtext to daily life, and God and guns run through public discourse like an electric current. Think of a place where influential scholars market theories of white supremacy, where the word 'liberal' is a negative epithet, where hang-'em-high law-and-order justice centered on the death penalty and throw-away-the-key sentencing are politically all but unstoppable. Think of a place obsessed with states' rights, as if it were the 1850s all over again and the Civil War had never been fought. Such characteristics have always described the South. Somehow, they now describe the nation."[8]

It is beyond surprising—it is staggering—what has happened. Growing up, we whites always said "the South shall rise again," and it now appears that the South has not only risen but has colonized great swaths of the American mind in the process. I have no clue where this story eventually ends, but right now the tale it tells is a sad one indeed. Among other unpleasant gifts, the South is a dominant force in a movement of radically reactionary politics that is leading our dear country into an era of tragic neglect or worse. Journalist Ronald Brownstein notes that "Nothing has contributed more to the conservative ascendancy in American politics than the realignment of the South from solidly Democratic to reliably Republican."[9] Of the 144 votes cast in the House of Representatives in October 2013 to continue the shutdown of the federal government and not raise the debt ceiling, 60 percent were from the South, all

Republicans. The South has led in voter suppression, antiunion right-to-work laws, same-sex marriage bans, executions, support for abundant military spending, and more.

Of course, there are many people in the South today who in varying degrees agree with these sentiments of mine and are working for change. They are proud of the South's positive contributions to national life, including those in music and literature, and proud also to see numerous communities in the South pioneering in the transition to a just and sustainable society. The Southern Grassroots Economies Project, for example, is promoting the development of cooperatives and worker ownership throughout the region. The South has its complement of progressive and compassionate souls, just not one large enough to set the cultural norms or regularly win elections, at least not yet.

Could it have been different? All along there have been powerful voices for something better. Most notably, there was Martin Luther King Jr. In 1963 on the National Mall he spoke the eloquent words: "I have a dream that one day on the red hills of Georgia sons of former slaves and sons of former slave-owners will be able to sit down together at the table of brotherhood. . . . I have a dream that one day in Alabama . . . little black boys and black girls will be able to join hands with little white boys and white girls as sisters and brothers. . . . This is our hope. This is the faith that I will go back to the South with."

One very different but very interesting plea for an alternative course came early on from the Nashville Agrarians, as Woodward mentions. Their manifesto, *I'll Take My Stand*, is a controversial collection of essays authored by a dozen Southern white men, published in 1930 on the eve of the Great Depression. These men were, it should be said, a distinguished group, mostly writers, poets, and academics—Allen Tate, John Crowe

Ransom, and Robert Penn Warren among them. They were mostly young—Warren was a Rhodes Scholar at Oxford at the time—and their ideas would later evolve in different directions.

In her preface to the seventy-fifth anniversary edition, Susan Donaldson wryly observes: "What is particularly striking as a recurring motif in essay after essay, though, is the self-portrait that is revealed almost in spite of itself, that of white southern men besieged by the forces of modernity, whether in the form of a dehumanizing market economy or by the prospect of regional memory and history being hijacked by those once defined as subordinates to white patriarchal control—that is, by white women and African Americans empowered by the forces of change."[10]

The Agrarians certainly did not get either race or gender right, and they saw in the South's agrarian history pretty much what they needed to see in order for the South to provide the counterpoint to the North's industrialization. But in their critique of the dominant American society they feared was taking over the South, they reached conclusions a lot like those being voiced today by critics of consumerism, materialism, GDP worship, environmental neglect, unfair labor practices, corporate power, and imperial designs—in short, by people like me.

I'll Take My Stand began with a "Statement of Principles" to which all twelve subscribed; the individual essays followed. It is well worth listening to what they had to say:

> The contribution that science can make to labor is to render it easier by the help of a tool or a process, and to assure the laborer of his perfect economic security while he is engaged upon it. Then it can be performed with leisure and enjoyment. But the modern laborer has not exactly received this benefit under the industrial regime.

His labor is hard, its tempo is fierce, and his employment is insecure. The first principle of good labor is that
it must be effective, but the second principle is that it
must be enjoyed. Labor is one of the largest items in the
human career; it is a modest demand to ask that it may
partake of happiness.   —STATEMENT OF PRINCIPLES

The producers, disguised as the pure idealists of progress,
must coerce and wheedle the public into being loyal
and steady consumers, in order to keep the machines
running. So the rise of modern advertising—along with
its twin, personal salesmanship—is the most significant
development of our industrialism. Advertising means
to persuade the consumers to want exactly what the
applied sciences are able to furnish them. It consults the
happiness of the consumer no more than it consulted the
happiness of the laborer.   —STATEMENT OF PRINCIPLES

The gospel of Progress is a curious development. . . . In
most societies man has adapted himself to environment
with plenty of intelligence to secure easily his material
necessities from the graceful bounty of nature. And
then, ordinarily, he concludes a truce with nature, and
he and nature seem to live on terms of mutual respect
and amity, and his loving arts, religions, and philoso-
phies come spontaneously into being: these are the
blessings of peace. But the latter-day societies have been
seized—none quite so violently as our American one—
with the strange idea that the human destiny is not to
secure an honorable peace with nature, but to wage an
unrelenting war on nature.   —JOHN CROWE RANSOM

The corporate form of our economic system makes possible a scale of exploitation unheard of in history.... Actually it is a form of legerdemain through which a stupendous concentration of wealth and power is achieved, along with a corresponding degree of exploitation of human effort. Centralization of political power and governmental regulation of industrial processes ... offer even greater possibilities of economic domination, because of the comparative ease with which control of government agencies is secured by industrial interests.... By "industrialism" is meant not the machine and industrial technology as such, but the domination of the economic, political, and social order by the notion that the greater part of a nation's energies should be directed toward an endless process of increasing the production and consumption of goods.   —LYLE H. LANIER

Any general policy of Southern industrial expansion should find discouragement through a consideration of the national and world aspects of industrialism, which has furnished the dominant motives and tools of modern imperialism. . . . The United States as a de facto empire is getting into a scramble for overseas markets, raw materials, and investment arrangements to complement industrialization at home in a way which makes Europe's pre-war scramble look small.
              —HERMAN CLARENCE NIXON

We of the minority see a law of diminishing returns in progress. . . . [T]his much is crystal-clear: our bigger-and-better society is now like a hypochondriac, so obsessed with its own economic health as to have lost the capacity to remain healthy....Nothing could be more salutary at this stage than a little healthy contempt for a plethora of material blessings. . . . The only thing . . . left out is whether the philosophy of industrial culture is not, in its ultimate development, irreconcilable with ecological conservation. I think it is. —ALDO LEOPOLD

Of course, I am being cute here. Leopold, writing in 1946 and 1948, was not part of the Agrarians, but, as one can see, much of his thinking parallels theirs, at least where the impact of so-called progress on nature is concerned.[11] That is even more true of the esteemed essayist and poet Wendell Berry, who has explicitly acknowledged his debt to *I'll Take My Stand*. In his essay "The Agrarian Standard," Berry states that "I believe that this contest between industrialism and agrarianism now defines the most fundamental human difference, for it divides not just two nearly opposite concepts of agriculture and land use, but also two nearly opposite ways of understanding ourselves, our fellow creatures, and our world."[12]

The South itself could never truly offer a viable alternative to America's dominant system of political economy, not then and not now, but in their rejection of that system, the Agrarians developed a well-ordered dissection of flaws that would only grow over time and that still today frame the case for a new system, a subject I take up in Part IV. All of which brings me full circle, so to speak.

I began writing to rediscover an era long lost to me and many others, and in the end I find a group of Southern white men whose critique of American society and economy circa 1930 is very similar to what I have set out in my recent books, at least that part of their thinking I have recounted here. I must give them that, and it is no small thing. There is a bit of worthy heritage reclaimed here that is useful for the future. The Agrarians had some extremely important things wrong, but they raised many valid concerns about where the country was headed—concerns that deserved an audience then and does so even more today.

The fast-growing sustainable food movement in America is the most visible manifestation of what my friend Courtney White and others are calling the new agrarianism. White, who founded and led the remarkable Quivira Coalition of ranchers and conservationists in the Southwest, sees the new agrarianism as an affirmation of life carried out in a particular place, sustaining the nature of that place both environmentally and culturally, with work and leisure mixed together well and with a healthy dose of self-provisioning.[13]

The agrarian in us is one reason Cameron and I found our way to rural Vermont. We have an ample garden, put in an orchard to complement the apple trees that are everywhere, and raise chickens and ducks. Even more, we are surrounded by farmers, woodlot managers, community-supported agriculture, food and other co-ops, farmers' markets, craftsmen, and wildlife. Just yesterday two orioles, fletched with an unimaginably beautiful orange, came visiting, joining the full menagerie of rose-breasted grosbeaks, goldfinches, bluebirds, turkeys, red-tailed hawks, indigo buntings, and others.

Part III

My life has been one great big joke,
A dance that's walked
A song that's spoke,
I laugh so hard I almost choke
When I think about myself.

MAYA ANGELOU

FIVE

Reflections
on a Résumé

I speak often at meetings and conferences these days, and when I am introduced, my hosts frequently comment on how impressive my résumé is. As my titles, awards, degrees, and more are recited, I sit there basking in the glow of accomplishments recounted, often remembering good things that happened along the way. Sometimes I even begin to believe my own write-up. So, before launching into more details of my career as an environmentalist in the chapters that follow, I want first to take a brief and sometimes lighthearted look at that résumé. Along the way, I'll point out things that happened in my various jobs that seem important today, things that resonate with me powerfully still.

Here is how a recent interviewer summarized my career: "His résumé is as mainstream and establishment as it gets: environmental advisor to Presidents Carter and Clinton, founder of the Natural Resources Defense Council and World Resources

Institute, administrator of the UN Development Program, dean of the Yale School of Forestry and Environmental Studies, now a professor at Vermont Law School, and distinguished senior fellow at Demos. . . . This elder environmental statesman is the author of the acclaimed books *Red Sky at Morning* (2003) and *The Bridge at the Edge of the World* (2008) . . . [and a] forceful new book, *America the Possible: Manifesto for a New Economy.*"[1]

That's all accurate, and it even skips a few things. But no one should ever mistake a résumé for reality. A small number of résumés contain outright fabrications and more gild the lily quite a bit. But these are not the real problem. The real problem is what they don't tell us, mine included.

When I take off my thick glasses and send my thoughts roaming back over my life, I am struck by three things: a lot of blind, dumb luck; a bevy of blessings in disguise, often rejections for which I am deeply thankful; and, most of all, the abundant efforts of others—family, friends, coworkers, colleagues.

I believe that those who have considered the matter view my time in the various positions I have held as generally successful. I know that I worked quite hard. But I want readers to believe me that I deserve only a sliver of whatever credit is due. Above all, the coworkers at the various organizations where I have served have been extraordinary. And Cameron has been a godsend at every turn—for her editing, her help finding compatible funding sources and hard-working board members, her support as a sounding board and advisor, and the emotional and spiritual texture that would not exist without her. When I was dedicating my last book, *America the Possible*, here is what I wrote: "For all those with whom I've had the privilege of working over these past four decades. If I could gather you in my arms, it would be a bouquet to save the world." I meant it and still do. And in the cases of NRDC and WRI, we were able to secure generous founding grants from two of America's private foundations, the Ford Foundation and the MacArthur Foundation. I do not mean to gush here, but I feel so remarkably blessed.

Noting that so much of the US economy depends on the efforts of others in the past, the Nobel economist Herbert Simon once quipped that if "we are very generous with ourselves, I suppose we might claim we 'earned' as much as one fifth of [our income]." That's about how I feel about that résumé of mine and, indeed, my life. *My* accomplishments? Hardly. We are carried forward by others—generous, caring, hard-working, and often loving people, angels by the river.

For me, the hinge of fate started bending right out of high school. Had I gone to MIT, which I almost did, I would likely have ended up as a scientist or engineer and thus would have had a very different story to tell. Had I not failed miserably at what I was trying hard to do for Gene McCarthy in 1968, I could easily have gone into "public life" in South Carolina and Lord knows where that might have led. Down the Appalachian Trail? And here is the weirdest of all "what ifs" for me to contemplate. What if Cameron and I had gone to coed colleges? Would we have stuck together as we did? I will insist the answer is "yes!" but acknowledge that it might have been more challenging.

As hard as we were trying, there was no certainty that our group at the Yale Law School would find funding for our dream of a public interest law firm for the environment, a dream that would eventually become NRDC. So, while I was clerking for Supreme Court Justice Hugo Black in 1969–1970, I started looking for another job. One stop was the Children's Defense Fund. I thought I would be irresistible, but I was promptly told, "no, sorry, we don't want you." Had CDF wanted me, I might have become a lawyer for children instead of the environment.

In fact, we worked very hard to make NRDC a reality, and we were successful. Apart from the common effort of building one of America's premier environmental advocacy organizations, what did I accomplish personally at NRDC that brings some pride today? Three things come especially to mind. First, we had a large hand in focusing public attention on the risks of the Atomic Energy Commission's breeder reactor and plutonium recycle programs. The AEC was projecting the construction of 400 breeder reactors by 2000, despite the extra safety and nuclear proliferation risks of this new type of nuclear reactor. Beyond that, the agency was seeking approval to proceed with the reprocessing of used nuclear fuel, extraction of the plutonium from the spent fuel, and use of that plutonium in new reactor fuel, despite the criticism that plutonium could be illegally diverted from this fuel cycle and used by nations or terrorists to make nuclear weapons. With the help of Margaret Mead, scientists Thomas Cochran and Dean Abrahamson, and attorney Anthony Roisman, we helped assure that both programs were ultimately terminated. Our world today is still vexed by the potential links between nuclear power and nuclear weapons, but these problems would have been much worse had the United States proceeded with what was referred to as the "plutonium economy."

My fellow NRDC cofounder Edward Strohbehn and I collaborated in bringing citizen suits to ensure full implementation of the new Clean Water Act. Through a series of lawsuits, and in the end with the enthusiastic cooperation of the Environmental Protection Agency, we were successful in having regulatory controls brought to a long list of toxic water pollutants that were not previously covered by the agency. Our agreement with the agency eventually became part of the federal water law.

The most controversial of the legal actions I initiated was the case that declared that the US Army Corps of Engineers had jurisdiction to protect wetlands associated with all US waters, not just the mostly coastal wetlands associated with traditionally navigable waters. Shortly after we won that one, the US Department of Agriculture and various farm and ranch groups intentionally kicked up a firestorm by announcing that millions of farmers and ranchers would now be required to get federal permits. The controversy continues even now, but the result we obtained that day in court has led to protections for countless freshwater wetlands.

After seven wonderful years at NRDC in the thick of the most important period in US environmental history, I left in early 1977 to join the Carter administration. I had done extensive volunteer work for the Carter campaign. My résumé says I was first a member then chair of the White House Council on Environmental Quality, and that's true insofar as it goes. What it doesn't say is that I was interviewed by President Carter for the position of administrator of the Environmental Protection Agency and that he passed over me for that position in favor of a far more suitable person who proved to be a great EPA administrator, Douglas Costle. Costle showed up every day in a conservative three-piece suit, knew a lot more about government and management than I did, and had an aura of calm competence—and the heart of an environmentalist. I would have made a mess of EPA, I'm sure of that.

The CEQ years were a challenge for me. Not only was I learning how to be effective in government, but I was also learning how to manage a staff, something I had not done before, and making some mistakes in the process. From the administration's point of view, I was a bit of a loose cannon. One year into Carter's term, the *New York Time*'s David Burnham wrote a story on how the president's appointees were faring. Asked to comment on that issue, Ralph Nader had this to say: "'There are some very good people in government now. But one-quarter of the President's term has slipped by and, with the exception of Gus Speth [a member of the Council on Environmental Quality], these people are not speaking out, not developing their constituencies, not publicly questioning the long-established policies of government,' he said." The *New York Times* noted that "Mr. Speth recently called on the Carter Administration to consider halting the construction of new nuclear reactors in a few years if the nuclear waste problem is not resolved."[2] The White House was not happy with my nuclear waste speech, and I had to explain myself to the president, quite literally. Carter was forgiving, but it was a close call.

I became more of an insider as the administration continued and after I was appointed CEQ chair. Thanks in major part to the little agency's outstanding professional staff, we helped Carter achieve a strong environmental record. At the conclusion of his term, CEQ and other agencies were asked to reflect on what had been accomplished. I replied in a memorandum to the president dated December 15, 1980: "From the perspective of environmental quality, yours has been an historic Administration. No President has done more." The memorandum went on to discuss the administration's many achievements, including permanent protection of vast natural areas in Alaska; the first ever federal initiatives to promote energy efficiency and renewable energy sources; important

Gus, as chair of the White House Council on Environmental Quality, meets with President Jimmy Carter. The council was among the first to urge national policy on climate change.

actions addressed to three critical problems resulting from the use of nuclear energy: weapons proliferation, radioactive waste management, and nuclear safety; a halt to the traditional "pork barrel" process for construction of federal water resources projects; pathbreaking attention to international resource and environmental challenges; enactment of the strong national law regulating stripmining; executive orders protecting wetlands and floodplains; and a series of tough antipollution regulations at EPA.

When I review the many issues in which I was involved at CEQ, one towers over all the others. Thirty-five years ago, we at CEQ were at the center of the first serious effort in the United States to move the climate change issue into the national policy arena and to urge an eventual halt to the buildup of greenhouse gases in the atmosphere.

Throughout the 1970s, as the sophistication of climate models improved, scientists in the United States, Japan, and elsewhere were growing increasingly concerned. By 1977 the National Academy of Sciences was sufficiently comfortable with the evolving scientific understanding to issue a report on the dangers of an unrestrained buildup of carbon dioxide in the atmosphere caused by fossil fuel use.

Then, in 1979, when I was CEQ chair, I was approached by Gordon MacDonald, a top environmental scientist and a former member of the council, and Rafe Pomerance, then president of Friends of the Earth. They were seeking my help in focusing the attention of both the Carter administration and the public on the issue. In early May, 1979, I followed up with a letter to MacDonald and George Woodwell, one of the country's top ecologists, asking them to cochair an effort to prepare an accessible, scientifically credible report on the problem, one that I could take to the president and others. By July the report was on my desk, signed by four distinguished American scientists— David Keeling and Roger Revelle in addition to Woodwell and MacDonald. Its contents were alarming. The report predicted "a warming that will probably be conspicuous within the next twenty years," and it called for early action: "Enlightened policies in the management of fossil fuels and forests can delay or avoid these changes, but the time for implementing the policies is fast passing."[3]

I soon presented the report to President Carter and others in his administration. The new Department of Energy reacted negatively. It was then promoting a massive program to develop liquid fuels from coal, tar sands, and oil shales. The report I had received pointed out that these "synthetic fuels" would produce even more climate-altering gases than conventional fuels. DOE promptly produced a counter-memorandum. Interagency disputes are an everyday affair in the federal government, but this one signaled the birth of an issue that has persisted unresolved for over three decades and now embraces the fight over the Keystone XL tar sands pipeline: Should the federal government be pursuing policies to break the hold of the fossil fuel industry on our country's energy policy, or should it continue to facilitate an ever deeper commitment to coal, oil, and natural gas?

Unknown to us at CEQ at the time, the president's science advisor, Frank Press, who was aware of where the latest science was pointing, had earlier asked the National Academy of Sciences to look hard at whether the new climate models were trustworthy and to assess the scientific basis for concern about man-made climate change. Massachusetts Institute of Technology scientist Jule Charney led the Academy review, and the "Charney Report" was published in late 1979. Its findings supported those in the report I had received at CEQ. The chair of the Academy's Climate Research Board summarized them: "The conclusions of this brief but intense investigation may be comforting to scientists but disturbing to policymakers. If carbon dioxide continues to increase, the study group finds no reason to doubt that climate changes will result and no reason to believe that these changes will be negligible. The conclusions of prior studies have been generally reaffirmed. However, the study group points out that the ocean, the great and ponderous flywheel of the global climate system, may be expected to slow the course of observable climatic change. A wait-and-see policy may mean waiting until it is too late."[4]

Emboldened, we at CEQ focused our most intense scrutiny on the issue of global climate disruption. By the time we left office in January 1981, CEQ had called for action on climate change in three public reports. Our most important report, a sophisticated analysis led by a brilliant CEQ scientist, James MacKenzie, was completed in the waning days of the administration. In my foreword to our report, released in January 1981, I sought to explain the climate disruption issue and its seriousness to a large audience:

"Atmospheric carbon dioxide plays a critical role in warming the earth; it absorbs heat radiation from the earth's surface, trapping it and preventing it from dissipating into space. As the concentration of carbon dioxide in the atmosphere increases, more of the earth's radiated heat is trapped. Many scientists now believe that, if global fossil fuel use grows rapidly in the decades ahead, the accompanying carbon dioxide increases will lead to profound and long-term alteration of the earth's climate. These climatic changes, in turn, could have far-reaching adverse consequences, affecting our ability to feed a hungry and increasingly crowded world, the habitability of coastal areas and cities, and the preservation of natural areas as we know them today. . . .

"Clearly, a deeper appreciation of the risks of a carbon dioxide buildup should spread to leaders of government and business and to the general public. The carbon dioxide problem should be taken seriously in new ways: it should become a factor in making energy policy and not simply be the subject of scientific investigation. Every effort should be made to ensure that nations are not compelled to choose between the risks of energy shortages and the risks of carbon dioxide. This goal requires making a priority commitment here and abroad to energy efficiency and to renewable energy resources; it also requires avoiding a commitment to fossil fuels that would preclude holding carbon dioxide to tolerable levels. Steps should also be taken to slow the disturbing global deforestation now underway, particularly in the tropics, and to encourage the regrowth of forests. . . .

"One imperative we share is to protect the integrity of our fragile craft and the security of its passengers for the duration of our voyage. With our limited knowledge of its workings, we should not experiment with its great systems in a way that imposes unknown and potentially large risks on future generations. In particular, we cannot presume that, in order to decide whether to proceed with the carbon dioxide experiment, we can accurately assess the long-term costs and benefits of unprecedented changes in global climate.

"Whatever the consequences of the carbon dioxide experiment for humanity over the long term, our duty to exercise a conserving and protecting restraint extends as well to the community of life—animal and plant—that evolved here with us. There are limits beyond which we should not go in disrupting or changing this community of life, which, after all, we did not create. Although our dominion over the earth may be nearly absolute, our right to exercise it is not."

The 1981 report was covered well in the media, despite our lame-duck status. America's leading environmental journalist, Philip Shabecoff, wrote in the January 14, 1981, *New York Times* that "The President's Council on Environmental Quality warned today that national and international energy policies must immediately start addressing the problem of carbon dioxide pollution if major long-range climatic and economic problems were to be avoided."[5]

Shabecoff noted that I, as chair of the council, "conceded that there was still some scientific uncertainty about the timing and effects of the carbon dioxide buildup in the atmosphere.

But Mr. Speth said that, given the magnitude of the risks and the fact that industrial countries were now formulating long-range energy plans, the carbon dioxide buildup must be considered in energy policy decisions."

The *New York Times* story noted that one recommendation of our report was "that agreement be reached by industrialized nations on a safe maximum level for carbon dioxide in the air. It suggested a level 50 percent higher than that of preindustrial times as an upper limit." In other words, we knew enough way back then, when there was plenty of time for effective action, to suggest that carbon dioxide be capped at not more than 420 parts per million (ppm), a limit that is not far off the mark given today's understanding. In 2013, carbon dioxide levels were already at 397 ppm and were climbing steadily. Only heroic national and international actions can now limit the buildup of greenhouse gases at a safe level, and many climate analysts now see little chance of that.

For more than three decades even non-geniuses like myself have known, or could easily have known, not only the gravity of the climate challenge but also more or less what to do about it. And, of course, little has been done. Efforts are now underway to achieve a new international agreement, but hardly anyone expects it to be an adequate response. Meanwhile, back home, Congress today is dead in the water, saddled as it is with a majority of Republicans in both houses self-identifying as "climate skeptics" or worse, with the result that the Obama administration is left with little but the 1970 Clean Air Act to do what it can, which if the president succeeds with the plans announced in June, 2014, should be, at long last, a start.

The world will not act vigorously on the climate issue without US leadership, and for over three decades that has been a scarce commodity indeed. The end result is beyond pathetic. It is probably the greatest dereliction of civic responsibility in the history of the Republic. Over the past century human societies have inflicted such devastating consequences on both people and planet that one must be cautious about superlatives, but surely the ongoing destruction of Earth's climate regime must rank at or near the top, certainly in terms of human folly and the resulting loss. It would be one thing if societies had unknowingly stumbled over some precipice, but the climate change tragedy already unfolding around us was entirely foreseeable.

Shortly before the American voters elected Ronald Reagan president in 1980, the position of dean of the Yale School of Forestry and Environmental Studies came open, and I believed that would be a great position from which to continue my environmental work after CEQ. Some members of the faculty there promoted that possibility with Yale's president, Bart Giamatti, and he invited me to Yale for an interview with him. Well, Bart turned me down and selected a fine man and an actual forester, John Gordon, instead. I also threw my hat into the ring for the presidency of Common Cause and had the pleasure of being interviewed by Watergate hero Archibald Cox, then Common Cause's chair. Had I gotten either of those jobs, I might not have pursued the effort to launch what became the World Resources Institute in 1982. WRI has been an invaluable actor internationally and nationally on environment and development issues. It is important that WRI was created, and I relate that story in the chapter that follows.

Looking back at my ten years leading WRI, I find it a challenge to select from our many actions what was most important and lasting. By 1987, WRI had an excellent staff of over fifty, and substantial policy research was underway addressed to essentially all the major global-scale environmental challenges. Soon thereafter, we would grow to include major programs in international assistance for sustainable development. It all seemed very important to me then, and still does. But if I had to choose one thing, it would be our persistent work on the climate change issue, which contributed importantly to putting the climate change issue on the international agenda and then to adopting the convention on climate protection signed at the Earth Summit in 1992. Unlike most other multilateral environmental agreements, the United States actually ratified that convention, though as I mentioned, our country did little subsequently to implement the agreement. The Obama administration now seems intent on starting to regulate carbon emissions from power plants, and I fervently hope it succeeds.

WRI also played a major role in developing the economics of sustainable development, and our focus on the systematic presentation in the *World Resources Report* series of hard data on conditions and trends internationally has proven invaluable around the world. Senator Robert Stafford, Republican of Vermont and then chair of the Committee on Environment and Public Works, summed up WRI's overall contribution when he wrote us that "More than any other non-governmental entity, the World Resources Institute has focused the attention of the public and decision-makers of the United States on the critical new environmental and resource issues of the 1980s."

Toward the end of my decade as president of WRI, I became excited about the idea of launching a new professional school for environmental management. I approached Dartmouth College about the idea; that seemed to me the ideal place for it. We had several good meetings on the subject, including a small conference at Dartmouth's Minary Center on Squam Lake. In the end, though we agreed on the concept, we couldn't come to agreement on financing. I wanted Dartmouth to put serious start-up money on the table, but they resisted. So we dropped the idea. I'm glad we did. As the national elections in 1992 took shape, I was highly motivated to help Bill Clinton and Al Gore get elected. I had worked with Gore when he was in the Senate, mostly on the climate issue, and greatly admired his leadership. So, I offered what help I could in the presidential campaign.

Right after the election, I was asked to head the natural resources-energy-environment-agriculture part of the Clinton transition in November and December. I took up that work with great enthusiasm and assembled a strong team to help get the new administration ready and to put together briefing books and other materials for the incoming cabinet members. But quickly the pushback started. First was Senator Bennett Johnson of Louisiana who called me to his office to complain that I had not consulted with him on energy matters and had not brought onto my transition team representatives from the oil and gas industry. Pretty soon I was hearing from politicians and lobbyists on behalf of many industrial and agricultural interests. Al Kamen started writing about me in his *Washington Post* column, In the Loop, referring to "the jolly green giant" who was running important parts of the Clinton-Gore transition.

One morning I received an interesting call from Senator David Pryor from Arkansas. He said to me, "Gus, I am very worried that you don't have any brawlers on your transition team!" "Brawlers, Senator?" I replied. "Our team can fight with the best Washington can offer." "No, son, you don't understand. Brawlers! The brawler industry." And then it became clear. He was talking about chickens. Broilers. Tyson Foods, Springdale,

Arkansas. "Yes, Senator. I'll speak with the National Chicken Council right away about sending someone over here."

Finally, I got a call from a member of Gore's staff. She said, "Gus, the Senator wants you to solve this problem for us." The problem, I gathered, was me—too green and arousing too many of America's anti-environmental interests. In the end, I think we did a fine job with our briefing books and other tasks. Many of the trade association representatives on our team proved quite helpful. I concluded they were mostly there to report back to their associations what was going on.

I know that Gore thought I could be of use in the administration, and I was mentioned as a possibility for a couple of senior appointive positions. But I think I had become more liability than asset in the eyes of some in the new administration. As the administration was staffing up, I was asked to provide a list of positions I would like to hold, in priority order. When I saw some positions on my list being filled by others, passed over again, I put something new at the top—the United Nations Development Programme. I had worked with UNDP while at WRI and had great admiration for the organization, the UN's principal agency for international development assistance. UNDP at that time was ably led by Bill Draper, and it was Bill who originally suggested to me to think about being his successor. Thanks to Gore, I got word in mid-1993 that the administration was recommending me to the Secretary-General to become administrator of UNDP. At that time the head of UNDP always went to an American, and I got the position.

Leading UNDP was the most intense, demanding, and educational job I ever had, and I loved it. I went to more than one hundred countries, both our donor countries and developing countries where UNDP had offices and assistance programs.

Had I got my original wish and gone into the Clinton administration, none of this would have happened. As I see it now, that
would have been unimaginably unfortunate.

There is a history of UNDP, Craig Murphy's *The United
Nations Development Programme: A Better Way?*, and it contains
a chapter about yours truly. It is mostly positive and compli-
mentary, but it is honest about the difficulties I faced and some
shortcomings on my part. On the positive side, Murphy writes
that: "Speth's face did, in a sense, become that of UNDP. . . .
He worked to make human development (with an additional
focus on environmental and institutional sustainability) the
operational framework of UNDP's programmes. Under Speth,
UNDP became an organization dedicated to just one thing:
'sustainable human development,' SHD. With a scholar's
thoroughness, Speth attempted to make the organization a
coherent instrument of this one purpose. That required adding
new capacities to deal with the environment, extreme poverty,
and those crises that rob people of the opportunity to pursue
human development. Sakiko Fukuda-Parr, who at the time was
a manager overseeing programmes in eleven of the poorest
African countries, recalls the exhilaration she and many other
officers felt as a result, 'I had something to work with, a purpose
that should be driving all the country programmes.'"[6]

The UN staff is often maligned, but I am among its defenders,
at least when I think of the dedicated professionals involved in
the world body's "operational activities" providing development
and humanitarian assistance in the world's poorer and con-
flict-ridden regions. Shortly after I arrived at the United Nations
in 1993, the director of the Office of the Administrator, Bruce
Jenks, (i.e., the person in charge of me) commented that "with
staff from all over the world, it's a wonder that it works at all." But

it does. I have been quoted more than once as referring to these staffers as "the last great gathering of idealists on the planet."

My visits to our program offices took me to the world's poorest and most dangerous places. I even signed an agreement on girls' schooling with the Taliban in Kandahar, though the Taliban adhered to it for only a short while. Almost everywhere I went for the United Nations I confronted a world of great suffering and deprivation, Keats's "the giant agony of the world." I had lived near true hardship in Orangeburg, of course, but had not really seen it. These UN experiences drove home to me that I have lived a life of comfort and plenty and have done little to deserve it, most of it occasioned by being born white and male to nice parents in mid-twentieth century America. The obscene disparities in economic and social conditions that we see both at home and abroad are the measure of the obligation that many of us share to be a force for change.

If leading UNDP itself was a wonderful opportunity, the other role assigned to me by Secretary-General Boutros-Ghali and later Kofi Annan, that of coordinating the UN's many development agencies, proved difficult, to put it mildly. "Herding cats" comes quickly to mind, but it was harder than that. Then, in 1997 Kofi Annan asked my friend Maurice Strong to lead a process aimed at reforming the UN's operations, including its development assistance activities, and I worked closely with him. Strong had ably orchestrated the two major UN conferences on the environment and sustainable development, and he knew the United Nations well. He was the ideal appointment to lead the reform effort, but even he found the sledding rough. There was no shortage of fierce infighting as agencies resisted any proposal that might diminish their independence. Thanks to Strong's leadership, important reforms were put in place in the end, including the creation of an overall coordinating structure, the UN Development Group, and the requirement that all UN development agencies work together in each country to forge and implement a common, shared program. I became the first chair of the Development Group.

One of the challenges I faced was raising funds for UNDP, especially in Washington. Because I was an American, the expectation was that Washington would be generous to UNDP and the United Nations generally. But that was not to be. Murphy explains that I "faced the most difficult fund-raising environment ever experienced by any Administrator with fund-raising skills that were probably no better than those of his predecessors. Certainly Speth would have had more credibility in the reform process had donors been increasing their contributions to UNDP."[7]

Financial support for UNDP from much of Europe was excellent. The Nordic countries were contributing about $16 per capita to UNDP, compared with the United States's 50¢ per capita. The big problem was Washington. Indeed, I left the United Nations in 1999 because I had come to believe that the European critics of Washington's poor support of the United Nations were right. The *Washington Post* correctly reported in April that year that "Challenges to American hegemony [at UNDP] surfaced in 1996 because of U.S. failure to pay financial obligations that the United Nations now claims amount to $1.6 billion and because the United States, traditionally the largest contributor to UNDP, cut its contributions that year from $113 million to $52 million. The United States since has boosted its donations back to an annual level of about $100 million.

"But the EU countries, which jointly contribute more than half of the UNDP budget, argued that the United States no longer is entitled to have its nationals at the head of UNDP as well as two other major U.N. aid agencies."[8]

To this day the United States remains a laggard when it comes to international development and humanitarian aid. Five to seven European countries typically meet or exceed the international goal of contributing 0.7 percent of national income as aid. America gives less than 0.2 percent, though it is the largest donor in absolute terms.

Although the European discontent with the United States was often framed in financial terms, the problem was deeper. In the late 1990s the United Nations had become a political whipping boy for many in Congress. Even the normally sensible Bob Dole campaigned against "the pale blue flag of the United Nations" in his 1996 presidential bid.

I did not leave the United Nations quietly. In April 1999 the *New York Times* reported on an interview I had given them: "With American debt to the United Nations soaring and contributions to development aid plunging, the outgoing chief of the United Nations Development Program, the highest-ranking American in the United Nations system, has accused the United States of 'tragic shortsightedness' in failing to support the world body.

"The United States has consistently 'undervalued, underutilized and underfunded' the United Nations and its agencies in recent years, said the development chief, James Gustave Speth, a soft-spoken environmentalist known to be close to Vice President Al Gore."[9]

When I left, the *New York Times* noted that, "Under Mr. Speth's tenure, the agency expanded its work significantly, from development projects in poor countries to broad involvement in fostering better government. The organization also encouraged private enterprise in countries where economies were stagnant because of extensive government control."[10] The article might have added the strong capability we had built to work on "complex emergencies," those country situations where social and political breakdown, civil disorder and armed conflict, and refugees all come together. When I got to the United Nations, Somalia was raging. The genocide in Rwanda occurred soon after. The conflict in Kosovo was ongoing when I was leaving. It was important work, but I knew it was time for me to move on.

After pursuing the idea of joining a professional environmental school twice earlier, the third time was indeed a charm. Thanks to Yale president Richard Levin and Frances Beinecke, a trustee of the university, Yale did circle back to me in 1998, and for a decade I had a great time as dean of Yale's environment and forestry school. If Yale had looked elsewhere again, I don't know what would have happened to me after the United Nations, but it is doubtful that I would have started writing books. I'm sure that my three books with Yale University Press are among the most important things I've done professionally.

There is a short piece I wrote while at Yale, though, that may be my best. It is not one of my books or cited articles, and it is relatively unknown, but it is one of the most important things I've written, at least if importance is judged in the abstract rather than in real-world impact. Here is how it came about.

I was two years into my deanship when 9/11 happened. In fact, I was riding Metro North from New Haven into the city to meet with Kofi Annan at the United Nations when the planes collided with the World Trade Center towers. As those of us in Grand Central Terminal were watching the horror unfold on TV, an announcement was made that the last and only Metro

North of the day would be departing promptly for New Haven. I jumped aboard.

Back at Yale the following day, I met with a group of students who were grief-stricken and wanted to talk. We sat together sharing our thoughts. Several students had tears in their eyes; all were greatly distressed. The loss was heavy with them, and I think in the background was a realization that the world had shifted beneath them. Their futures had been affected, and not positively.

After that meeting I wanted to write something for the Yale students, something that would show a positive path forward from 9/11. And so I did. It just poured out. My years in the United Nations had enabled me, when need be, to see the world as a non-American might and that helped. One week after 9/11 on September 18, the *Yale Daily News* published my essay. I want very much to rescue it from obscurity because to this day I believe it points to the course America should have taken, a course very different from the one we did in fact take. Nearby I reproduce the essay I sent to the student newspaper. Knowing what has happened since 9/11, I find it hard to read without joining those Yale students in tears. Like the climate change issue, We Should Have Known Better.

If I had difficulty raising money for my UN agency, I redeemed myself at Yale. I was able to identify a group of remarkable, generous individuals who shared both a love for the university and a love for the environment. With their help, and the help of the school's impressive faculty and staff, we were able over a decade to add fifteen new faculty positions, double the size of the average scholarship, increase by 50 percent both the number of students applying and the number of courses offered, carry out a ton of high-quality research and

writing, launch a world-class online environmental magazine, and construct a new, super-green home for our school,
Kroon Hall. That marvelous structure has won over a dozen
top architectural awards, including being selected as one of the
top ten green buildings in the world by the American Institute
of Architects. Our architects deserve great credit, but Kroon
Hall would not have happened without my Yale colleagues
Stephen Kellert and Alan Brewster, who nurtured the project
with insight and determination on a daily basis. Yet, beyond
all these accomplishments is the most important thing we did:
reaching 1,500 exceptional young people with an empowering
educational experience.

Have I made my career seem like an accident? That was
very far from the case. There were certainly avenues that did
not open up and turns I did not take. At several points I hedged
my bets. Life is full of contingency, and I have been extremely
fortunate in how things actually worked out. But in truth I was
an ambitious cuss, determined and stubborn. I knew what I
wanted, and I planned very carefully and worked hard to get
NRDC started, to secure the appointment to CEQ, to launch
WRI, and to become head of UNDP. In the end, and thanks to
help from others, I got the jobs I really sought. The two most
difficult and protracted efforts—the launching of the Natural
Resources Defense Council and the World Resources Institute—
could not have happened without extraordinary colleagues, as
I will relate shortly.

After four big assignments for which I had advanced
myself and my causes, I remember wondering, when I was at
the United Nations, whether I would ever receive an offer out
of the blue for a position I really wanted. And then, near the
end of my six years at UNDP, it finally happened. At a UN event

she was also attending, Frances Beinecke approached me about becoming dean of Yale's environment school. Not only did they want me, but they were willing to wait a year for me. After promoting myself so vigorously, I have to say that was a great feeling. I got that feeling again when the Vermont Law School invited me to join its outstanding faculty and top-ranked environmental law program. I am happily ensconced there still.

When friends comment on the number of positions I've held, I often reply, "Couldn't hold a job, I guess." More seriously, I have worried about losing steam if I stayed too long in a position. There comes a point when you have done what you can do, or most of it, and I've believed it's important when that time comes to clear out and make space for one's successor.

In my case, one thing led to another. Opportunities that I could put my heart into opened up, and I went for them. The biggest theme that has run through the six serious jobs I've held is, of course, the environment, but—and this is one thing I hope my young readers will appreciate—when I started at NRDC in 1970, I didn't know much at all about either environmental science or environmental policy. So my advice is, put yourself ahead of the curve, and go for it. Trust yourself to succeed. It's odd, but dreams are the firmest foundation.

There is, of course, a lot more to life than a career—things a résumé never documents. Catherine was born in 1969, Jim in 1972 and Charlie in 1976, and Cameron and I had three decades of hands-on parenting. Now they are all educated, meaningfully employed, married to delightful spouses, happy, and parenting themselves, with two kids each. From the late 1970s on, our family passion has been hitting the road together bound for some beautiful destination, starting with the Boundary Waters Canoe Area Wilderness and, most recently, all fourteen of us gathering in the Tetons. Dan Jenkins refers to "life its ownself" in his humorous book by that title, and the Speth family has had its full share of it. Our family has been a tremendous inspiration to me, and a source of more joy than anything in my résumé. But that, as they say, is another story.

MAKING THE WORLD SAFER, WITHOUT BOMBS

From the *Yale Daily News*, September 18, 2001

Many Yale students with whom I have spoken want to look beyond a war on terrorism, as important as that is. They are seeking something more positive and constructive to rise from the ashes in New York and Virginia.

It is already possible to envision the broad outlines of a positive agenda—one that befits a great nation and a caring people, and one that differs in many respects from the call to arms now being repeated like a drumbeat. Beyond the overt and covert anti-terrorist operations that will, and should, be mounted lie a range of more difficult and subtle challenges that must be addressed if we are serious about confronting terrorism and its roots.

Understanding and meeting these challenges can be an enormous contribution of your generation. No generation will be more affected by the events of last week than yours, and no generation can do more to help our country draw the right conclusions from Tuesday's tragedy and take the right steps in light of them.

1. Principled and intelligent conduct in the war on terrorism

In our effort to eliminate terrorist cells around the world, we should not abandon the current U.S. ban on state-sponsored assassinations. We have found this practice abhorrent, and the principle was not changed by last week's tragedy. Similarly, whether we are operating at home or abroad, we cannot abandon our commitment to human rights and civil liberties, our tolerance of differing viewpoints or our acceptance of religious and ethnic diversity.

Also important is a measured and careful approach to anti-terrorist operations. *New York Times* columnist Thomas Friedman has correctly observed that those who attacked us are in fact hoping to trigger a massive U.S. retaliation that makes no distinction between Muslim terrorists and other Muslims, thus inciting the entire Islamic world against us. We must not become "Osama bin Laden's chief recruiter," Friedman noted.

2. Goodbye to American unilateralism

The Bush administration has walked away from international agreements and out of international meetings; it has shown disdain for the views of our closest allies on issues such as missile defense; it has proceeded as if the only country worth wooing was Mexico. Yet success in the war on terrorism will depend totally on international cooperation and not just from OECD countries.

The positive agenda here is to shift American policy away from the go-it-alone mentality that has guided the administration's policy both in defense and energy and toward collaborative engagement and cooperation with the rest of the world. More broadly, it is past time for the American public to outgrow its self-centered and isolationist tendencies and to become more aware of and sophisticated about international affairs.

3. Superpower with humility

In a thoughtful piece in Sunday's *New York Times*, John Burns wrote from Islamabad that "To be free, rich and powerful in a world that is mostly none of these things is, inevitably, to engender resentments."

We can find a hundred ways—in government, business and our personal contacts—to show our respect for other cultures, especially Islamic ones; we can take seriously claims that economic globalization is proceeding too fast and without regard to local communities or social and cultural values; and we can conduct ourselves in all spheres with less arrogance and more humility and with new interest in non-economic values and objectives.

4. Dialogue on Islam and Islamic governments

Terrorists exist in America, East Asia, Europe and, indeed, almost everywhere, but radical Islam obviously poses a special challenge. A two-pronged effort at dialogue is needed. In one, responsible Islamic leaders and people of good will everywhere should seek to isolate and delegitimize those who would cynically pervert Islam to justify and motivate terrorist behavior.

As Friedman noted, there is a civil war within Islam between the modernists and the medievalists, and we should do everything possible to strengthen the hand of the former.

In the other dialogue, we must challenge the governments of the Arab states and predominantly Islamic countries to move to greater openness and democracy and to opt for greater investments in the human development of their own people. We can support these goals with real assistance, as indicated below.

5. Reconsideration of specific U.S. policies

A major source of Arab-Islamic animosity toward the United States is a reinforcing set of specific policies that should be reassessed: a seeming insensitivity to the Palestinian perspective, uncritical support of autocratic Arab governments, the stationing of U.S. troops in Saudi Arabia and the U.S.-sponsored economic sanctions against Iraq.

The question in each case is to see if a new balance can be found which addresses the offending policies while still protecting essential U.S. interests, including our commitment to the security of Israel.

6. Focus on development and democracy

Dealing with terrorism requires identifying and addressing underlying conditions that can constantly replenish the supply of bin Ladens and suicide bombers. Among these conditions are the poverty and hopelessness in which recruits are found. Widespread hopelessness in a world of extraordinary wealth and luxury leads easily to bitterness, anger and the capacity for violence. In the Arab states today, levels of human deprivation are even higher than one would predict from income levels.

Hopelessness can be overcome, for example, by measures that invest in the United Nations' Millennium Goals, which seek major improvements in global health and education and access of the world's poor to assets that can empower them economically, socially and politically. Eliminating mass poverty in the lifetimes of today's undergraduates is an achievable objective.

Yet the United States has turned away from its historic commitment to helping the world's poor and is now dead last in the OECD in providing development assistance in comparison with its GDP. In my six years in the United Nations, I found America is now known for lecturing the world, not for its generosity.

If we have something to give to the world, other than democracy and the Bill of Rights, it is the opportunity for the half of humanity that lives on less than $2 a day to have a better life and participate in increasing prosperity. That will require new policies and new generosity on debt relief, development assistance, trade access and foreign investments—policies that are well understood by those interested in conquering world poverty but thus far largely ignored by the United States.

The above agenda is by no means complete nor is it free of risks and conflicting objectives. But it does help point us toward a different role for America in the world. The caring and generosity and selflessness so evident in America in the wake of last week's attacks must not be confined to the home front but must be extended abroad.

Somehow out of all the sorrow and loss must come discovery of a new national identity: an identity that seeks the great things for which our country has always stood—democracy, opportunity and equality before the law—not only for ourselves but for all the world's citizens.

Part IV

Whither is fled the visionary gleam?
Where is it now, the glory and the dream?

WILLIAM WORDSWORTH

SIX

The Greening

*E*ntering my third and final year of law school at Yale, after a summer working for Senator Gene McCarthy with little to show for it, I was fast shedding my thought of a political life in South Carolina. In a year, I would graduate and my twenty-one years of formal education would end. I would then have to go out into the real world. What was I to do with myself?

The third year of law school, as most law students come to appreciate, is not a time when you learn much more about the law. But it is a time you can learn something about yourself. The prospect of having to decide on a career, or at least start one, can concentrate the mind. And so it did. In the fall of 1968 the big law firms sent impressive individuals to interview at Yale, and I accepted several invitations. But I knew I did not want to go with a big firm. Higher on my list was the possibility of teaching at Princeton's Woodrow Wilson School of Public and International Affairs, and that fall I was invited down for an interview. Moreover, I must not have gotten the idea of heading South totally out of my system: In October I wrote the Southern

Regional Council in Atlanta about job possibilities. And I also did what many of the most aspiring law students do: I applied for a judicial clerkship, in my case with Supreme Court Justice Hugo L. Black. My mentor and friend, Yale Law professor Charles Reich, for whom I was working as he was writing his remarkable *The Greening of America*, had clerked for Justice Black, and Reich graciously wrote Black a letter recommending me.

It was about this time, in October of 1968, that I had an important idea. Perhaps it is too grand to call it an epiphany, but I tend to think of it that way. I was riding the New Haven Railroad into New York City reading the *New York Times*, and I read one story about the NAACP Legal Defense Fund's litigation, and a story about an environmental issue caught my eye. Lawyers are trained to think by analogy, and it hit me: Get a group of my impressive classmates together and start a public interest law firm for the environment!

Events then moved quite rapidly. Every fellow student I asked to join the group accepted, so we had to tell others who wanted to join with us to sit tight and wait. Lawyers, perhaps particularly Yale lawyers, tend to believe we can do anything, and it never occurred to us to doubt that we could do the job. But it did occur to us that we might not find the money and that, if we got too big, finding the needed funding would be even harder.

At that point in the history of American environmentalism, there was hardly anything called environmental law, and Yale offered no courses in the field. To the best of my knowledge, neither did any other law school. We anticipated using common law a lot—tort and nuisance law, the public trust doctrine, and property and land-use law. But I did identify one attorney in New York City who practiced environmental law. Numerous people told me: go see David Sive. So I went to visit him in his law office. David had a back injury at the time, and he was obviously in pain, but he was supportive of our idea and encouraging. He mentioned something that turned out to be crucial. He said, "Do you know, recently someone was seated in that same chair that you are in whose name is Frank Barry? He's been asked by the Ford Foundation to do a study of the creation of exactly what you're talking about." So I said, "Well, could you tell me how I could reach Frank Barry?"

He did, and I contacted Barry and asked him, after we had talked a couple of times, to come to Yale to meet with our group and some Yale faculty. He expressed great interest in that, and he did come, on November 11. Apparently he liked what he saw, and that led to our connecting with the Ford Foundation. I will always be thankful to Sive and to the three Yale Law professors who took a risk and threw their great prestige behind us, vouching for us with the Ford Foundation: Boris Bittker, Charles Reich, and John Simon.

Our group quickly jelled and worked together well, often meeting around our dining room table, as Cameron reminds me. By the end of November, we had a name—several actually, but let's use Legal Environmental Action Fund (LEAF) here—a letterhead, the first draft of a funding proposal, a rough start-up budget, drafts of articles of incorporation and bylaws, and a list of prospective board members. Soon we were in serious and encouraging conversations with the key people at Ford, and in March 1969 we submitted a formal proposal to the foundation. Our intrepid team—which included Richard Ayres, John Bryson, and Edward Strohbehn—had had a good few innings. We discovered along the way that Ford was interested in public interest law generally as well as in environmental protection, so that different units of the foundation were working together for the same ends.

It was soon clear to us at Yale that if we were to receive Ford support, it would not come in time for us to launch the organization right out of law school. So our group was glad we had sought other post-graduation opportunities. In November I heard from Justice Black that he wanted me to clerk for him for the 1969 term of the court. What a pleasure it was to work with that great man. Among other things, I was there to lend a hand when "the Judge," as he was known to his clerks, wrote in a 1969 Circuit Justice opinion that he would seek to end the days of "all deliberate speed," the vague timeframe prescribed for ending segregation in *Brown v. Board of Education*, and to declare that racial segregation must end "now." The following month, shortly after the court's term began, the full court agreed.

Part of the answer of what I could do with myself was provided by a different route altogether: I would be a father! In April 1969 Cameron gave birth to our first child, the adorable Catherine. At that point we were living in a cottage surrounded by magnificent trees on the banks of Lake Quonnipaug in North Guilford, Connecticut. It was spectacular in so many ways that spring. Cameron, who had been putting me through law school working as the Master's secretary in one of the Yale residential colleges, retired to tend to our new baby, the lake was lovely, the flowers were in bloom, none of us were taking the last semester of law school seriously, my clerkship with Justice Black was all lined up, and we had just submitted our funding proposal to the Ford Foundation. I have been extremely happy many times in my life, and this was one.

A year later Catherine could walk, and on a fine Washington, D.C., spring day very close to her first birthday, she toddled proudly in her white smock through the crowds on the National Mall for the first Earth Day. It was really that year, the first year of Catherine's life, that the modern environmental movement in America was born.

Launching LEAF hit some snags in the period after law school. Early in my clerkship with Justice Black, in October of 1969, I wrote Reich reporting on the status of our effort and our recent conversation with Ford president McGeorge Bundy: "LEAF is not doing too well . . . Bundy has told us to get lost until the foundation tax legislation passes both houses." [That legislation would end up having a profound impact on the way Ford and other foundations can operate, and Bundy did not want to further rock the boat.] I went on: "Apparently [Congressman] Wilbur Mills personally wrote Bundy two letters complaining about our group specifically, and Bundy also caught it from other foundations worried that Ford was endangering the whole foundation world by funding us. Our problem now is that we have to bide our time until the legislation clears and by then our group might be split. Also, the people at Ford might not be as interested in us then as they were last spring. There's still hope, of course, and we intend to keep trying to get some funding, if not from Ford then from elsewhere. But things are not as bright as they once were."

That was the low point, but things soon got better. We were blessed by having several highly credible scientists and others step forward to vouch for us, people like ecologist George Woodwell, who was senior scientist on the staff of Brookhaven National Laboratory. Then, the foundation legislation I mentioned in my letter to Reich became part of the Tax Reform Act of 1969. When the foundation issues were settled in Congress, we beat a fast track back to the Ford Foundation. The foundation had a surprise for us. To provide us youngsters "cover," they wanted us to merge with another of their grantees, a Washington, D.C.-based group focusing on urban issues. At this point we had broadened our four-member Yale group to include a Harvard Law grad, the very able Thomas Stoel. Stoel and I looked into the group recommended by Ford. Stoel was never one to mince words, and I'll always remember the look on Bundy's face when he reported that the urban group "was going down a rat hole." Indeed, they did close down shortly thereafter.

Around this time, Ford was approached by another group with an idea similar to ours. This new group, which was already incorporated as the Natural Resources Defense Council, was led by two senior Wall Street attorneys, Whitney North Seymour and Stephen Duggan. They had just been involved in a landmark legal effort to save the Hudson Highlands' Storm King Mountain from a pump storage power plant. They had hired a young man with litigation experience, John Adams, to be executive director. Ford told both of us that they would provide start-up funding if and only if the two groups would merge. This was not what we had in mind. Not a boss! Not a Wall Street board! We, the "Yale group," as we had come to be known, did some soul searching and had some disagreement among ourselves, but in the end all of us decided to explore the merger idea and see what we could make of it.

I met with Seymour in mid-January of 1970, and then we met with John Adams later that month. We were trying to get to know each other, but we were also negotiating on matters like board composition and participatory decision making. Here is how John describes what happened in the book he did with his wife Patricia in 2010, *A Force for Nature*:[1] "Gordon Harrison and Ned Ames of the Ford Foundation had informally promised us $350,000 a year for three years, but only if we could work out an agreement with the Yale group. This did not come easily. The Yale law students were young and brash, outraged at what they saw as the crimes of corporate America and very suspicious of anyone from Wall Street. 'I don't know if we can survive these guys,' I often said to Patricia. 'They can be such a pain in the ass. And if anyone refers to Mr. Duggan again as grandpa.' . . .

"However, Gus Speth had the foresight to see what we could accomplish as a single organization, and he was anxious for us to join forces. In March 1970, we assured the Ford Foundation that we would do just that. We had succeeded in uniting two very different groups and styles—the aggressive initiative of the Yale group and the seasoned experience of 'establishment' lawyers and old-style conservationists. Together we would bring about change within the system: I thought of what we were doing as 'responsible militancy.'"

John and Patricia captured my views correctly, but they give me too much credit. Ayres, Bryson, Strohbehn, and I all favored becoming a single organization. In March 1970, I wrote the Ford Foundation telling them that we were prepared to merge efforts, and NRDC did the same. We had fallen in love with John Adams. I have a note I wrote in February 1970 that says about him: "He is a pleasant, easy going guy who should be easy to work with. He does not appear to have any interest in monopolizing control, abusing his position, or preventing us from pursuing the objectives we originally set out for LEAF." Adams turned out to be a great leader. He would stay at the helm of NRDC for thirty-six years and near the end of it would be awarded the Presidential Medal of Freedom, the nation's highest honor.

We thought we were home free, but unbeknownst to us a member of the Nixon White House staff, Tom Charles Huston, who would become well-known later for the Huston Plan—the

The NRDC staff celebrates their breeder reactor victory in 1983. *Left to right:* nuclear program director Tom Cochran, cofounder and trustee Gus Speth, senior attorney Barbara Finnemore, cofounder and executive director John Adams, and international program director Jacob Scherr.

domestic surveillance plan made infamous by Watergate—had sent the president a memo dated June 18, 1969, which said: "Some weeks ago, the Committee of Six recommended that we explore the possibility of getting the IRS to take a close look at the activities of left-wing organizations which are operating with tax-exempt funds. You approved our recommendation. After some delay, Dr. Burns and I have finally had an opportunity to discuss the matter with [IRS head] Randolph Thrower . . . I think it is vital that we put the brakes on some of these foundations which are busy financing leftwing causes with the tax payer's money. Certainly we ought to act in time to keep the Ford Foundation from again financing Carl Stokes' mayoralty campaign in Cleveland."

In reply, Nixon wrote aide Arthur Burns, "(1) good— (2) But I want action. Have Huston follow up hard on this." And so with new IRS restrictions on the granting of tax exemptions under section 501(c)(3) of the Internal Revenue Code in place that spring, who should walk through the door with its application for exemption? Yep, NRDC. The IRS refused to grant us the tax exemption and thus ensued a fierce policy battle that lasted through the summer and into the fall. In the end, in November of 1970, the IRS capitulated, and NRDC got its exemption, paving the way for Ford's founding grant to NRDC.

I have to hand it to the Ford Foundation. Despite having Congressmen Wilbur Mills and Wright Patman as well as President Nixon after them, they persisted and funded not only NRDC but also the Environmental Defense Fund, the Center for Law and Social Policy, the Center for Law in the Public Interest, and other groups that have made extraordinary contributions. The foundation launched a new era of public interest law and advocacy in America.

With the Ford grant securely in hand, Bryson, Strohbehn, and I moved to Washington, D.C., to start the NRDC office there. Ayres stayed in the New York headquarters. We were finally in business. David Sive, Charles Reich, Boris Bittker, and George Woodwell all served on the founding board of trustees. Today NRDC has a budget of over $100 million a year. A mighty oak, it has been said, is just a little nut that held its ground.

My friend and former dean of the Vermont Law School, Jeff Shields, said to me recently that there is a deeper story of this period that I must tell. "Why did you strike out in the direction you did when most law graduates went into private or government practice?" he asked. "How does your story relate to America's story?" I think Jeff was right that it is important to understand the birth of the modern environmental movement in America and, in particular, to understand the debt those of us who were "present at the creation" of modern environmentalism owed to the civil rights movement through which we had just lived. Yes, we were bright ambitious young law students looking for something different and interesting to do with ourselves. But we were also midstream in a series of important currents in American history, part of an era worth recalling, for, as I will try to explain, that recalling can inform and instruct today.

We were children of the 1960s. Our Yale group had entered college as the civil rights movement was in full swing; we became antiwar as the US troops in Vietnam escalated; though unfortunately all male, we were glad to see the birth of the National Organization for Women in 1966; and though we were not hippies or drop-outs, we shared much of the counter-culture's critique of American society.

As Charles Reich's research assistant as he was finishing *The Greening of America*, I agreed with what his best-selling 1970 book had to say:[2] "In the second half of the twentieth century [the] combination of an anachronistic consciousness characterized by myth, and an inhuman consciousness dominated by the machine-rationality of the Corporate State, have, between them, proved utterly unable to manage, guide, or control the immense apparatus of technology and organization that America has built. In consequence, this apparatus of power has become a mindless juggernaut, destroying the environment, obliterating human values, and assuming domination over the lives and minds of its subjects." I know that I was highly motivated to correct the societal flaws that Reich had cogently identified in his book and in his class, which I took. We were not among the radicals of the 1960s, but we were talented lawyers who could use our skills to help right some terrible wrongs.

We shared the 1960s sense of hope and the desire to bring about serious change in American society. We had studied the civil rights litigation and other important cases, and we knew the importance of the law and good lawyering in the public interest. We had seen the impact of social movements, of citizens standing up and speaking out. We knew from the civil rights legislation and otherwise that our government in Washington could do great things, in addition to getting us into great wars, and indeed that government was essential if great things were to be done. The 1960s had taught us that activism could succeed, that government could succeed. We were 1960s idealists, for goodness sake. None who went to NRDC wanted to go to a law firm, and there were plenty more like us. We could have easily recruited another entire staff from the Yale Law School Class of 1969. Indeed, another nine Yale lawyers from our era would eventually join NRDC.

All this youthful energy and hope and idealism we poured into the environmental cause. There is a passage at the beginning of Thomas Hobbes's *Leviathan* where he describes the courtyard geese alerting those inside to an intruder "not because they were they, but there." That is not quite how it was with us and the environment. We were predisposed to the environmental cause, and did not take it up merely because it was an emerging national concern and thus a wonderful opportunity for us to do some good in the world. But, looking back, it is also true, I think, that we went pell-mell into environmental advocacy in part because we anticipated that the new issues "were there." I know that in my case I believed I had largely missed one great American struggle, civil rights, and I did not want to miss another.

Though one might not appreciate it today, the American environmentalism of the 1960s and early 1970s was rather radical. Reality was radicalizing. Pollution and blight were blatant and obvious to all. Smog, soot, smarting eyes, coughs from air pollution; streams and beaches closed to fishing and swimming; plastic trash and toxic chemicals that would not go away; birds, even our national symbol the bald eagle, threatened by DDT; pesticide poisoning; fish kills; power plants and highways through neighborhoods; marshes filled for new tract houses; and streams channelized for navigation and drainage. The view that major corporations were getting away with murder was widespread. Rachel Carson published *Silent Spring* in 1962 and Ralph Nader wrote *Unsafe at Any Speed* in 1965. The antiwar movement had an influence, too. For example, Senator Gaylord Nelson, aware of the teach-ins to protest the Vietnam War, had the idea for a national teach-in for the environment and thus launched, with the fine help of Denis Hayes, what became that first Earth Day in 1970.

When the Santa Barbara oil spill occurred in 1969, a citizens' committee there issued this powerful declaration reminiscent of earlier ones in the 1960s on different issues: "We, therefore, resolve to act. We propose a revolution in conduct toward an environment that is rising in revolt against us. Granted that ideas and institutions long established are not easily changed; yet today is the first day of the rest of our life on this planet. We will begin anew."

Many of the nation's leading environmental thinkers and practitioners of the period concluded that deep societal changes were needed. GDP and the national income accounts were challenged for their failure to tell us things that really matter, including whether our society is equitable and fair and whether we are gaining or losing environmental quality. The most forceful challenge to our GDP fetish can be found in Robert Kennedy's last major speech, in 1968. A sense of planetary limits was palpable. *The Limits to Growth* appeared in 1972 and sold over a million copies. Its authors and others saw a fundamental incompatibility between limitless growth and an increasingly small and limited planet. Scientists Paul and Anne Ehrlich and John Holdren in 1973 argued for an economy that would be "nongrowing in terms of the size of the human population, the quantity of physical resources in use, and [the] impact on the biological environment."[3] Joined with this was a call from many sources for us to break from our consumerist and materialistic ways—to seek simpler lives in harmony with nature and each other. These advocates recognized, as the Ehrlichs and Holdren put it, that with growth no longer available as a palliative, "one problem that must be faced squarely is the redistribution of wealth within and between nations." They also recognized the importance of creating employment opportunities by stimulating employment in areas long underserved by the economy and by moving to shorter workweeks. And they saw that none of this was likely without a dramatic revitalization of democratic life.

Digging deeper, ecologist Barry Commoner was not alone in asking "whether the operational requirements of the private enterprise economic system are compatible with ecological imperatives." Commoner's answer was "no." He believed that environmental limits would eventually require limits on economic growth. "In a private enterprise system," he wrote in his 1971 bestseller, *The Closing Circle*, "the no-growth condition means no further accumulation of capital. If, as seems to be the case, accumulation of capital, through profit, is the basic driving force of this system, it is difficult to see how it can continue to operate under conditions of no growth."[4]

It was these and similar ideas that motivated me during my initial years at NRDC. Yes, I had opted to work within the system, but I believed that legal advocacy could change the system. I believed that what I was doing was on the path to deeper change.

Throughout the 1960s and 1970s, awareness of environmental degradation was growing. In fact, it was hard not to be aware. The environmental problems of the day were in your face and in your backyard, and I saw them rooted in a wider set of maladies. When the opportunity came to do something about it, it came not as a stranger but something half expected, known, and welcomed.

I left NRDC in 1977 to become a member of the Council on Environmental Quality (CEQ) in the Carter White House, and that is where my second adventure in building environmental institutions began. That adventure grew out of the need to address the global-scale environmental concerns that were then belatedly coming into focus. These global concerns were a central part of our work at CEQ. As I mentioned, we issued several hard-hitting reports addressing the threat of global climate change.

The need for an independent policy center focusing on global-scale environmental and resource concerns became apparent to me as we at CEQ were finishing the *Global 2000 Report to the President* in 1980. It was a powerful report ably prepared by an interagency team led by Gerald Barney. The report highlighted the ongoing march of a dozen grave challenges—desertification, deforestation, climate change, species loss, ozone layer depletion, and more. The issues on the environmental agenda of the 1970s tended to be domestic and acute. *Global 2000's* agenda was international, and the issues less blatant but more threatening and more difficult. President Carter, running for reelection in 1980, was urged to distance himself from the report—"too much bad news already." But instead, to his credit, he championed it.

These global-scale problems were on my mind when I met with Carter on February 29, 1980, a few hours before the Second Environmental Decade celebration we had planned for that afternoon. Despite my fervent wish that people believe to the contrary, my meetings with the president were not frequent. So I took the occasion to brief him on matters other than the afternoon's event, including global resource and environmental issues.

I got quite a shock that afternoon. Toward the end of his speech to the two hundred or so guests in the White House's East Room, the president moved casually into a few paragraphs that were certainly not in the text on which we had been working: "Just before lunch, Gus and I were discussing the long-term threats which just a few years ago were not even considered." As if we often chatted about world developments before lunch! He then proceeded to review, quite eloquently, a number of these threats, and concluded on an optimistic note: "the last decade has demonstrated that we can buck the trends."

I remember thinking in 1980 that we in the United States were building a fool's paradise with our narrow focus on our domestic concerns. A new force was needed to broaden the scope of American environmentalism. It occurred to me, as it had with NRDC, to find some talented, highly regarded people, raise the needed funding, and launch a new center aimed at putting these global-scale issues on the map by using compelling analyses and outreach to the media. I had a chance to share the conclusions of *Global 2000* and my thoughts on next steps with a group of foundation leaders in New York in the fall of 1980, shortly after our defeat in the November elections. I remember worrying after that luncheon whether I had been sufficiently convincing. I also wondered what the MacArthur Foundation was planning. It was on the attendee list, but I had never heard of it.

Two months later, as I was packing my office items to make way for the Reagan administration, I received a telephone call from my friend Robert Socolow, a physicist at Princeton. Socolow said that the newly created MacArthur Foundation had someone on its board, a friend of his and another physicist, Cal Tech professor Murray Gell-Mann, who was taking the lead for the foundation in exploring possible support for pathbreaking policy studies. Gell-Mann was looking for someone to help the foundation with global-scale resource and environmental issues. Given my work on *Global 2000* and my imminent joblessness, Socolow thought I might be interested.

My heart was racing as I began my first call with Gell-Mann in late January 1981. He said the MacArthur Foundation wanted to investigate what should be done to address issues like those covered in *Global 2000*, and asked if I could lead it. I replied that I would love to work with him but that I was already set on building and leading a new policy-engaged think tank in that area. I wondered aloud whether I might have a conflict of interest. Gell-Mann replied, "That's okay. We can work with that," and it was the beginning of a beautiful friendship.

The institute project quickly became my highest priority, but it seemed like a longshot with MacArthur. Gell-Mann stressed that the foundation would have to be first convinced of the value of policy studies and then convinced of the priority importance of resource and environmental issues (in competition with other issue areas). Only after that would the questions of whether to spend and how much to spend and on what projects to spend even come up. The MacArthur board had a healthy skepticism, he said, and the idea of the foundation funding the start-up of a new institute was only a distant possibility. We agreed that the two initiatives—the

MacArthur exploration and the new institute proposal—
should be kept distinct.

By April, I had prepared a proposal for a new institute, and I
sent it to Gell-Mann. The first paragraph of my note to him was
as follows: "You asked recently what I thought *ought* to be done
in the resources and environment studies area. The enclosed
memorandum describes briefly a proposal I and others have
developed. The memorandum was developed independently
of your question and of my work for the MacArthur Foundation, but it does nevertheless provide a direct answer to your
question. I would like very much to have your thoughts and
suggestions concerning it."

The prospects were looking pretty bleak that spring, but I
was given encouragement and support to continue by some
wonderful people, none more so than John Adams at NRDC
and Thomas Jorling, who was then the director of Williams
College's environmental studies program.

The turning point came at the conference I organized for
the foundation in May 1981. A lot happened in Chicago in those
three days. The conversation with the MacArthur directors
advanced to the point that on the final day we discussed the
pros and cons of a distinct institution, funded by foundations,
for policy studies in the environmental area. The idea that
MacArthur could provide the initial funding was put forward,
without reply. One important upshot of the conference was
the MacArthur board's request to me to prepare a report for
the foundation that would sketch out the new institute idea
in greater detail. They wanted to see what I was talking about.

I will always be grateful to those who came to Chicago that
day and lent their support. I remember the powerful comments
offered by Elizabeth McCormack, George Woodwell, Jessica

Mathews, and John Adams, and there were others. Mathews was impressive as a scientist on the staff of the National Security Council in Carter's White House. Later that year, I asked her if she would leave the *Washington Post* and join the World Resources Institute (WRI) as vice president and research director. In January 1982, I was able to inform MacArthur that the project had acquired an enormously able vice president. Soon after, I also spoke with the rock-solid Wally Bowman about joining WRI as vice president for operations, and he agreed as well. We had our initial leadership team, and together we assembled a stellar board of directors led by former Undersecretary of State Matthew Nimetz and including leaders like Robert McNamara, Alice Emerson, Russell Train, and Ruth Patrick.

Though it took a year and a half of hard work by Jessica, Wally, Murray, and me, in May 1982, the World Resources Institute received a $15 million founding grant from MacArthur. Gell-Mann, who had won the Nobel Prize in physics for his work in understanding the subatomic world (he defined the quark and named it), told me that shepherding that grant through the foundation was the hardest thing he'd ever done! Over the years WRI has had a huge impact. Thanks to the great efforts of Mathews and Bowman and that of other staff members such as Robert Repetto, Mohamed El-Ashry, Janet Brown, Patti Adams, Alan Brewster, Rafe Pomerance, Andrew Maguire, James MacKenzie, Kathleen Courrier, Alan Miller, Irving Mintzer, and Marjorie Beane, all there in 1987, we had a big hand in bringing global-scale environmental challenges to the fore and helping to shape international responses. Patti Adams was my administrative assistant for a decade at WRI, and before that at NRDC and CEQ. Always thoughtful and helpful, I cannot imagine anyone better. I know that these are just names to some readers, but I place them here with great admiration, and there were others. When I think of them, I am reminded of Jean Giono's statement that "For a human character to reveal truly exceptional qualities, one must have the good fortune to be able to observe its performance over many years."[5] And I did.

Those were heady days, with high hopes and great expectations. The expectations have not been realized, however. The natural world is gravely threatened today, far more than in 1970, sad to say. I will take the next two chapters to explain what I think happened and what should come next. That said, I am glad that we have saved some of it. While at NRDC, I brought lawsuits under the Clean Water Act and the National Environmental Policy Act in several efforts to save wetlands in particular. As I mentioned earlier, through litigation and public campaigning, NRDC had a major hand in extending the Clean Water Act's protections to freshwater wetlands. We also halted the Department of Agriculture's extensive ditching of small rivers and streams and draining their swamps and marshes. While doing this work, I thought often of South Carolina's rivers and swamps and my many fishing trips on the Edisto with my father. Thanks to the work of countless environmentalists in and out of government, many wetland areas have been protected across our country, as powerful a testimony as any to the value of America's environmental community.

Like many others, Cameron and I are drawn to those precious wetland areas where land and water meet. We were fishing not long ago in the salt marshes behind the barrier islands northeast of Charleston, South Carolina. It was hot and humid as it always is in the summertime there, and the calm water was perfectly flat and glassy. Several dolphins surfaced around our boat, breaking the stillness. A hundred yards away, a brown pelican watched from atop a post that marked a channel. Oystercatchers gathered on the shell banks exposed by the tide. A great blue heron stood motionless peering into the shallow waters near the marsh grass. Mullet were jumping not far from the great blue. It was hard to leave, but the tide was going out, and soon there would be mudflats where we were. We didn't catch any fish that day, but it didn't matter, not much anyhow.

On a fine fall day for another outing, we drove across Vermont to a wildlife management area near Lake Champlain, hoping to find the migrating snow geese heading south. We heard them first, and then there they were, thousands of them feeding and resting in a cornfield and on the marshy banks of Dead Creek. Stretching across almost the entire horizon to the southwest, these magnificent creatures from the tundra were a joy to behold. We climbed up onto the car for a better view and watched for about an hour. Then, just when we'd decided to go check out the ducks and mergansers, the geese suddenly levitated en masse. In only a few seconds they were high in the sky, honking and whirling in ever-widening circles. We thought at first that they were heading off again on their journey, but slowly they descended on another rich area of corn and water. It was one of the finest sights I'll ever see, and I was reminded of John James Audubon's description of flocks of passenger pigeons darkening the sky.

It was a moment of hope as well as pleasure, seeing nature still strong despite all the wounds we have inflicted. But, as we stood there, it grew on me that this grand display was made possible not only by Mother Nature but also by people and their government, state and federal, acting together decades ago to create Vermont's Dead Creek Wildlife Management Area. They cared enough to create something wonderful for future generations, the work of angels we shall never see.

SEVEN

Environmentalism at the Crossroads

*A*lmost a half century has flown by since we launched the Natural Resources Defense Council. Over that period NRDC and other mainstream US environmental groups have racked up more victories and accomplishments than we can count. One shudders to think what our world would be like had they not.

Yet, despite those accomplishments, a specter is haunting American environmentalism—the specter of failure. All of us who have been part of the environmental movement in the United States must now face up to a deeply troubling paradox: Our environmental organizations have grown in strength and sophistication, but the environment has continued to go downhill. The prospect of a ruined planet is now very real. We have won many victories, but we are losing the planet.

Here we are, forty-four years after the burst of energy and hope at the first Earth Day, headed toward the very planetary conditions we set out to prevent. Indeed, all we have to do—to destroy the planet's climate, impoverish its biota, and toxify its people—is to keep doing exactly what we are doing today, with no growth in the human population or the world economy. Just continue to release greenhouse gases at current rates, just continue to degrade ecosystems and release toxic chemicals at current rates, and the world in the latter part of this century won't be fit to live in. But human activities are not holding at current levels—they are accelerating, dramatically. It took all of human history to grow the $7 trillion world economy of 1950. Now, we grow by that amount in a decade, even with today's slower growth rates.

How could this have occurred? Past is prologue, and to understand what happened to American environmentalism, we need to look at where we've been and how we got to where we are today—to tell the environmentalist's story. To anticipate the story's conclusion, recall that I said in the previous chapter that in launching NRDC we set out to change the system. But we didn't. We improved the system in places, made it safer, better. But in doing so we became part of the system. It changed us.

It must be hard for young people, from today's vantage point, to imagine what it was like to be an environmental advocate in the 1970s. But let me try to recapture that period.

First of all, it was a lawyer's heyday. The Clean Air and Clean Water Acts are perhaps the most forceful federal legislation ever written, and there they were, with their deadlines and citizen suit provisions, along with the National Environmental Policy Act, just waiting to be litigated and enforced. And we could not lose. NRDC won almost every lawsuit we brought. The judges were with us. NRDC had so many successful lawsuits against

EPA that an EPA assistant administrator said to me one day, "You know, you guys are running the agency."

Second, the environmental agencies were as gung-ho as we were. Some EPA staff would quietly point out how their efforts were being stymied by the Office of Management and Budget and hint at needed lawsuits. The Council on Environmental Quality in the White House was 100 percent reliable—a friendly environmental ombudsman within the government. The old-line agencies like the Department of the Interior were struggling to catch up, and, when they didn't, they were sitting ducks for our litigation.

In those early years, in the 1970s, economists were not seriously involved in setting environmental policies. We environmentalists initially ignored their calls for pollution taxes and market mechanisms, which infuriated some of them.

We think of our US environmental legislation as the product of the movement launched on Earth Day 1970, but that is not quite how it was. The National Environmental Policy Act passed in 1969; the Clean Air Act completed its passage through Congress in 1970. They were driven more by far-sighted legislators like Edmund Muskie (D-ME) and John Sherman Cooper (R-KY) than by environmental lobbying or even public pressure. I can say firsthand that we at NRDC had a hard time keeping up with what Muskie and his staff were doing in the development of the Clean Water Act. There was actual leadership in the Congress, and it was bipartisan. So we did not see the need then to build political muscle and grassroots support. The key politicians were already with us. Congress was actually leading.

Next, there was little organized opposition from the business community or anyone else. They were caught off guard, at least initially, though it did not take long for the opposition to materialize.

We saw little need in those years for getting into electoral politics, building grassroots strength, and supporting local groups, or even for environmental education. There was a wealth of intellectual and political capital and public support. And we were in a rush to get the job done!

Relatedly, there was no overall strategy among environmental groups, few metrics to gauge our success, and no objective but friendly environmental think tanks serving as watchdogs, assessing us, and pointing the way forward. (The Conservation Foundation filled some of this need for a while.) And environmental law and policy as it evolved was decidedly ad hoc, lacking a foundation of overarching and broadly supported principles.

Environmental law as it was created in the 1970s was federal law. Our view of the states and the cities was disdainful. They had done so little. It was time for Washington to take control, as had happened with civil rights. We were also not much interested in international conservation efforts. They seemed to be mostly talk, and we had plenty to do at home.

In the media, the environmental beat was hot, attracting the best reporters. The media overall were powerfully supportive. None of us of this era can forget CBS's anchor Walter Cronkite and his ongoing series "Can the World Be Saved?"

I think readers will sense where this story is headed. What happens when all that support in Congress weakens or even turns hostile, and we have neglected to build grassroots support and to get into electoral politics?

What happens when we have lived so thoroughly within the Beltway and submerged so completely in the staggering complexity of the regulatory mess we have helped to create, that we—wonkish us—cannot effectively communicate to a broad public, cannot strike those notes that resonate with average Americans and their hopes, fears, and dreams? What happens when we have elevated head over heart and lost the vernacular in favor of enviro-jargon like Prevention of Significant Deterioration, Corporate Average Fuel Economy Standard, Total Maximum Daily Loads, and the like?

What happens when we begin to confront a mighty opposition not just from a now alert corporate America but equally from an antigovernment, antiregulation, antitax coalition of ideologically driven right wingers, and we have centered all our plans on powerful action by the federal government and neglected to develop an equally powerful grassroots force and to build strength at the state and local levels?

What happens when the antiregulation forces come together to build a skilled messaging machine and we do not?

What happens when we need, but don't have, metrics to point out that we're winning victories but losing the war and when we need, but don't have, an independent think tank capacity to build new intellectual capital and to help us figure the way out of the mess in which we find ourselves?

What happens to the prospects for judicial remedies when half the federal judges are appointed by conservative Republican presidents? And when the environmental story no longer attracts the best reporters, the media lose interest, and the five corporations that control most of the media prefer to hear "both sides" even when "balance" becomes a form of bias?

And what happens when we find that economic issues have taken center stage and we have tended to neglect the economics profession and done too little to pioneer new ways of thinking about economics or the economy? And what happens when central pillars of our work—making the polluter pay, stopping this and that development—actually do raise prices and cost certain jobs at a time when half the country is just getting by, living paycheck to paycheck, economically insecure, and we have not forged powerful links with working people and their representatives and their research centers, and we are stuck with the reality that the only way we can save the planet is to show that it helps the economy and GDP?

What happens when those 1970s grade-schoolers grow up and know distressingly little about the environment or science? Only about half of Americans know how long it takes the earth to go around the sun!

And what happens when those hard-charging government agencies lose their luster and their drive and some become partly or wholly captives of those they are supposed to regulate?

What happens, of course, is what has happened. Progress slows down. Major resources shift from offense to defending past gains. New issues, like climate change, can't get traction.

So I think it is clear that the mainstream environmental organizations (with my participation) are partly responsible for the situation in which we found ourselves. There were major strategic adjustments needed but not made; new institutions and new arrangements should have been forged but were not. We carried on under President Reagan much as we had under President Carter, but the world had shifted under our feet. Recently, our mainstream environmental groups have begun to make adjustments, but they are very partial adjustments and, as I say, late.

While we environmentalists are partly responsible, it is decidedly the lesser part. To chronicle the much larger part of the blame, it is useful to begin with Frederick Buell and his valuable book, *From Apocalypse to Way of Life*. He writes: "Something happened to strip the environmental [cause] of what seemed in the 1970s to be its self-evident inevitability. . . . In reaction to the decade of crisis, a strong and enormously successful anti-environmental disinformation industry sprang up. It was so successful that it helped midwife a new phase in the history of US environmental politics, one in which an abundance of environmental concern was nearly blocked by an equal abundance of anti-environmental contestation."[1]

The disinformation industry that Buell notes was part of a larger picture of reaction. Starting with Lewis Powell's famous 1971 memo to the Chamber of Commerce urging business to fight back against regulations, well-funded forces of resistance and opposition have arisen. Powell, then a corporate attorney who would become a Supreme Court justice, urged corporations to get more involved in policy and politics. Virtually every step forward has been hard fought, especially since Reagan became president. It is not just environmental protection that has been forcefully attacked but essentially all progressive causes, even the basic idea of government action in the interests of the people as a whole.

As federal environmental laws and programs burst onto the scene in the early 1970s, we pursued the important goals and avenues those laws opened up. There, the path to success was clear. But we left by the wayside the more difficult and deeper challenges highlighted by Commoner, Ehrlich, and others forty years ago in the writings I mentioned in the previous chapter. And our gains in the 1970s locked us into patterns of environmental action that have since proved no match for the system we're up against. Ironically, these patterns were set in part by our own early successes, which were made possible in large measure by Senator Edmund Muskie and his remarkable aides Leon Billings and Thomas Jorling and their monumental air and water legislation. These new laws created major opportunities for lawyers and others to make large environmental gains, but in doing so we were drawn ever more completely inside the D.C. Beltway. Once there, inside the system, we were compelled to a certain tameness by the need to succeed there. We opted to work within the system of political economy that we found, and we neglected to seek transformation of the system itself.

I first developed my critique of today's mainstream environmentalism in 2008 in my book, *The Bridge at the Edge of the World*. The book also included prescriptions for new environmental strategies. Now, six years later, I can update and broaden that analysis.[2]

First, here is what I mean by working within the system. When today's environmentalism recognizes a problem, it believes it can solve that problem by calling public attention to it, framing policy and program responses for government and industry, lobbying for those actions, and litigating for their enforcement. It believes in the efficacy of environmental advocacy and government action. It believes that good-faith compliance with the law will be the norm and that corporations can be made to behave.

Today's environmentalism tends to be pragmatic and incrementalist—its actions are aimed at solving problems and often doing so one at a time. It is more comfortable proposing innovative policy solutions than framing inspirational messages. These characteristics are closely allied to a tendency to deal with effects rather than underlying causes. Most of our major environmental laws and treaties, for example, address the resulting environmental ills much more than their causes.

In the end, environmentalism accepts compromises as part of the process. It takes what it can get.

Today's environmentalism also believes that problems can be solved at acceptable economic costs, and often with net economic benefit, without significant lifestyle changes or threats to economic growth. It will not hesitate to strike out at an environmentally damaging facility or development, but it sees itself, on balance, as a positive economic force.

Environmentalists see solutions coming largely from within the environmental sector. They worry about the flaws in and corruption of our politics, for example, but that is not their professional concern. Similarly, environmentalists know that the prices for many things need to be higher, to reflect the true costs of goods and services, and they are aware that environmentally honest prices would create financial burdens for the half of American families that just get by. But the government action needed to address America's gaping economic injustices is not seen as part of the environmental agenda.

Today's environmentalism is also not focused strongly on political activity or organizing a grassroots political movement. Electoral politics and movement building have played second fiddle to lobbying, litigating, and working with government agencies and corporations.

A central precept, in short, is that the system can be made to work for the environment. Not everything, of course, fits within these patterns. There have been exceptions from the start, and recent trends reflecting a broadening in approaches are encouraging, especially the increased activism outside the Beltway as groups, including mainstream ones, have strengthened their political operations and grassroots networks. But, still, our principal environmental groups are slow to adjust to the new realities.

America has run a forty-year experiment on whether mainstream environmentalism can succeed, and the results are now in. The full burden of managing accumulating environmental threats has fallen to the environmental community, both those in government and outside. But that burden is too great. The methods and style of today's environmentalism are not wrongheaded, just far too restricted as an overall approach. Indeed, we badly need major efforts to work within the system, to make the system respond, which sometimes it does. The problem has been the absence of a huge, complementary investment of time, energy, and money in other, deeper approaches to change. And here, the leading environmental organizations must be faulted for not doing nearly enough to ensure these investments were made.

The environmental problem is actually rooted in defining features of our current political economy. An unquestioning society-wide commitment to economic growth at any cost; a measure of growth, GDP, that includes everything—the good, the bad and the ugly; powerful corporate interests whose overriding objective is to grow by generating profit, including profit from avoiding the environmental costs they create; markets that systematically fail to recognize environmental costs unless corrected by government; government that is subservient to corporate interests and the growth imperative; rampant consumerism spurred endlessly by sophisticated advertising; social injustice and economic insecurity so vast that they empower often false claims that needed measures would slow growth, hurt the economy, or cost jobs; economic activity now so large in scale that its impacts alter the fundamental biophysical operations of the planet—all these combine to deliver an ever-growing economy that is undermining the ability of the planet to sustain human and natural communities. Yet very few of these issues are addressed by US environmental law or mainstream environmental organizations.

It's clearly time for something different—a new environmentalism. And here is the core of this new environmentalism: It seeks a new economy. And to deliver on the promise of the new economy, we must build a new politics. New environmental leaders will learn from the ideas of the 1960s and early 1970s, rediscover environmentalism's more radical roots, and step outside the system in order to change it before it is too late.

We must ask again the basic question: What is an environmental issue? Air and water pollution, yes. But what if the right answer is that an environmental issue is anything that determines environmental outcomes. Then, surely, the creeping plutocracy and corporatocracy we face—the ascendancy of money power and corporate power over people power—these are environmental issues. And more: The chartering and empowering of artificial persons to do virtually anything in the name of profit and growth—that is the very nature of today's corporation; the fetish of GDP growth as the ultimate public good and the main aim of government; our runaway consumerism; our vast social insecurity with half the families living paycheck to paycheck. These are among the underlying drivers of environmental outcomes. They are environmental concerns, imperative ones, but they rarely appear on the agendas of our main national environmental groups.

We also need to address a second question: What's the economy for, actually? I will return to this question in the chapter that follows, but the answer, I believe, is that the purpose of the economy should be to sustain, restore, and nourish human and natural communities. We should be building a new economy that gives top, overriding priority not to profit, production, and power but rather to people, place, and planet. Its watchword is caring—caring for each other, for the natural world, and for the future. Promoting the transition to such a new economy must be the central task of a new environmentalism. It is a task that obviously cannot be accomplished by environmentalists alone but only by a powerful fusion of progressive and other forces coming together to build a new politics.

This new politics must, first of all, ensure that environmental concern and advocacy extend to the full range of relevant issues. The environmental agenda should expand to embrace a profound challenge to consumerism and commercialism and the lifestyles they offer, a healthy skepticism of growthmania and a redefinition of what society should be striving to grow, a challenge to corporate dominance and a redefinition of the corporation and its goals, a commitment to deep change in both the functioning and the reach of the market, and a powerful assault on the anthropocentric and contempocentric values that currently dominate American culture.

Environmentalists must also join with social progressives in addressing the crisis of inequality now unraveling America's social fabric and undermining its democracy. In an America with such vast social insecurity, economic arguments, even misleading ones, will routinely trump environmental goals.

Similarly, environmentalists must join with those seeking to reform politics and strengthen democracy. What we have seen in the United States is the emergence of a vicious circle: Income disparities shift political access and influence to wealthy constituencies and large businesses, which further imperils the potential of the democratic process to act to correct the growing income disparities. Environmentalists need to embrace public financing of elections, new anticorruption ethical restrictions on legislatures, the right to vote, tougher regulation of lobbying and the revolving door, nonpartisan Congressional redistricting, and other political reform measures as core to their agenda.

The new environmentalism must work with a progressive coalition to build a mighty force in electoral politics. This will require major efforts at grassroots organizing, strengthening groups working at the state and community levels, and both supporting and fielding candidates for public office. It will also require developing motivational messages and appeals. Our environmental discourse has thus far been dominated by lawyers, scientists, and economists. Now, we need to hear a lot more from the poets, preachers, philosophers, and psychologists.

Above all, the new environmental politics must be broadly inclusive, reaching out to embrace union members and working families, minorities and people of color, religious organizations, the women's movement, and other communities of complementary interest and shared fate. It is unfortunate but true that stronger alliances are still needed to overcome the "silo effect" that separates the environmental community from those working on domestic political reforms, a progressive social agenda, human rights, international peace, consumer issues, world health and population concerns, and world poverty and underdevelopment.

The final goal of the new environmental politics must be, "Build the movement." We have had movements against slavery and many have participated in movements for civil rights and against apartheid and the Vietnam War. Environmentalists are still said to be part of "the environmental movement." We need a real one—networked together, protesting, demanding action and accountability from governments and corporations, and taking steps as consumers and communities to realize sustainability and social justice in everyday life.

Can we see the beginnings of a new social movement in America? Perhaps I am letting my hopes get the better of me, but I think we can. Its green side is visible, I think, in the surge of campus organizing and student mobilization occurring today, including the efforts to get colleges and universities to divest from fossil fuel companies. It's visible also in the increasing activism of religious organizations and the rapid proliferation of community-based environmental initiatives. It's there in the occasional joining together of organized labor and environmental groups. It is visible in the green consumer movement, particularly in the efforts to move beyond consumerism. It's there in the increasing number of demonstrations, marches, and protests, including those focused on tar sands, fracking, mountaintop removal, and other energy and climate issues. It is there in the constituency-building work of minority environmental leaders, in the efforts of groups to link social justice and environmental goals, and in the efforts now underway to dethrone GDP and find new measures of progress and well-being. It's beginning, and it will grow. Over time, its principal driver will be climate change.

Only an unremitting struggle will drive the changes that can sustain people and nature. If there is a model within American memory for what must be done, it is the civil rights revolution of the 1960s. It had grievances, it knew what was causing them, and it also knew that the existing order had no legitimacy and that, acting together, people could redress those grievances. It was confrontational and disobedient, but it was nonviolent. It had a dream.

EIGHT

"'Ultimate Insider' Goes Radical"

*H*ow did a nice, conservative, Southern white boy become a civilly disobedient, older, still white guy bent on transformative change to a new system of political economy?

The people I know with any ambition want to be successful at what they do—to feel they are accomplishing something meaningful. And so we accommodate in various ways to what is required to be effective in the particular circumstances in which we find ourselves. It's important, then, to try to stay in jobs or other situations where that accommodation is not too much of a stretch. If it is, unless we're unusually malleable, we're going to be either unhappy or ineffective or both.

I have been extremely fortunate in this regard. I've held both advocacy and management positions that allowed me to stay comfortably in my own progressive skin, with ample freedom to maneuver. That said, it is true that those positions have all been jobs within the American mainstream, and true also that I conducted myself to be effective in those contexts. Thus it happened in 2004 that *Time* magazine referred to me as "the ultimate insider." I had never thought of myself that way, but it stuck and was picked up yet again in 2012 by Wen Stephenson in the title for an interview he did with me in the online *Grist*, titled "'Ultimate Insider' Goes Radical."[1]

Stephenson introduced the interview by noting my "soft South Carolina drawl," and pointing out that I am "nobody's picture of a radical," before adding:

"And yet this elder environmental statesman . . . has grown ever more convinced that our politics and our economy are so corrupted, and the environmental movement so inadequate, that we can no longer hope to address the climate crisis, or our deep social ills, by working strictly within the system. The only remaining option, he argues . . . is to change the system itself. And that, he knows full well, will require a real struggle for the direction and soul of the country.

"Which is why . . . he was arrested in front of the White House on Aug. 20 [2011]—along with Bill McKibben and eventually more than 1,200 others—in an act of nonviolent civil disobedience protesting the Keystone XL pipeline."

That modest act of nonviolent civil disobedience landed us in the central cellblock of the District of Columbia jail for three days. I went to jail with Bill McKibben and scores of others because I found myself at the end of my proverbial rope. After more than thirty years of unsuccessfully advocating for government action to protect our planet's climate, civil disobedience was my way of saying that America's economic and political system has failed us all.

The journey from "insider" to "radical" that Stephenson describes began when I returned to Yale in 1999. My decade-long tenure as dean of the Yale School of Forestry and Environmental Studies provided me the opportunity to step back from the fray and do what professors are supposed to do: take a hard, searching look at what is actually going on. Subsequently, the Vermont Law School provided the same opportunity. At both I not only had the time to reflect but also the freedom and encouragement to speak out. That was part of the job, not a hindrance to it.

Shortly after becoming dean, I began looking at information on conditions and trends in the environment and, later, in other areas to see where America actually stands after several decades of much progressive effort and even more resistance. And the harder and longer I looked, the more I felt that I was being mugged by reality. As I noted earlier, after years of claiming this and that environmental victory, we find ourselves today fast approaching environmental catastrophe. More broadly, if one looks at where the United States stands among the twenty leading advanced democracies on thirty key indicators of national well-being—poverty, inequality, education, social mobility, health, environment, and on and on—you find that "We're Number One!" in exactly the way we don't want to be—at or very near the bottom. So I started organizing my thoughts, offering lectures, and then writing.

My first sustained effort to articulate my growing concerns was *Red Sky at Morning: America and the Crisis of the Global Environment*, published by Yale University Press in 2004. It grew out of a series of lectures I had given in a course for Yale undergraduates. For over twenty years prior I had worked to promote international responses to a series of pressing global-scale problems: climate change, biodiversity loss, ozone depletion, deforestation, desertification, and more. By the time I took a group of Yale students to the World Summit on Sustainable

Development in Johannesburg in 2002, the international community had in fact adopted an impressive array of treaties and
other agreements addressed to almost all these challenges. My
first task was to assess how these agreements were working. I
was prepared for some bad news, but it was worse than I anticipated—and not much has changed in the decade since 2004.
As I wrote in *Red Sky at Morning*, "the bottom line is that these
treaties and their associated agreements and protocols do not
drive the changes that are needed. Thus far, the climate convention is not protecting climate, the biodiversity convention
is not protecting biodiversity, the desertification convention is
not preventing desertification, and even the older and stronger
Convention on the Law of the Sea is not protecting fisheries.
Nor are they poised to do so in the immediate future. The same
can be said for the extensive international discussions on world
forests, which never have reached the point of a convention. . . .

"It would be comforting to think that all of the international negotiations, summit meetings, conference agreements,
conventions, and protocols at least have taken the international
community to the point where it is prepared to act decisively—
comforting but wrong. Global environmental problems have
gone from bad to worse, governments are not yet prepared to
deal with them, and, at present, many governments, including
some of the most important, lack the leadership to get prepared."[2]

Those conclusions forced me to ask *why*. What had gone
wrong? My answer was that, "the failure of green governance
at the international level is a compound of many elements.
The issues on the global environmental agenda are inherently
difficult . . . powerful underlying forces drive deterioration and
require complex and far-reaching responses, while the inherently weak political base for international action is typically

overrun by economic opposition and protection of sovereignty. Meanwhile, the response that the international community has mounted has been flawed: the root causes of deterioration have not been addressed seriously, weak multilateral institutions have been created, consensus-based negotiating procedures have ensured mostly toothless treaties, and the economic and political context in which treaties must be prepared and implemented has been largely ignored. To some degree these results can be attributed to accidents, errors, and miscalculations, but the lion's share of the blame must go to the wealthy, industrial countries and especially to the United States."[3] The United States gave strong leadership in the effort to protect the ozone layer but after that became a big part of the problem in international negotiations. In effect, I concluded, the international community brought weak medicine to a very sick patient.

There are deeper drivers of deterioration than our treaty regimes are addressing—the root causes that I mentioned. *Red Sky at Morning* identified ten: population growth, mounting affluence, inappropriate technology, widespread poverty, market failure, policy and political failure, the scale and rate of economic growth, the nature of our economic system, our culture and its misguided values, and the forces loosed upon the world by the globalization of the economy. This, obviously, is quite a list. Undaunted, I went on to propose an agenda for real change in global environmental governance, including what is needed to address these ten underlying forces. So little has since been done to adopt my proposals that, a decade later, they are for the most part still as fresh as a daisy.

The book was getting attention, but I was not satisfied with my first effort to get to the bottom of the environmental problem, and I wanted also to broaden the analysis beyond the global-scale challenges and to focus particularly on the United States. When the opportunity arose to offer the DeVane Lectures at Yale, I accepted the invitation and decided to use the lectures as the means to explore these issues more deeply. There's nothing quite like the requirement of delivering a fresh, hour-long lecture every week for a semester in front of two hundred people to concentrate the mind, and in the winter and spring of 2007, that's what I did. *The Bridge at the Edge of the World*, published the following year, was the product of those lectures.

The breakthrough for me was to see those root causes and underlying drivers of deterioration as aspects of a system, and *The Bridge at the Edge of the World* named it: population growth and poverty in the developing world were factors, I concluded, "but the much larger and more threatening impacts stem from the economic activity of those of us participating in the modern, increasingly prosperous world economy. This activity is consuming vast quantities of resources from the environment and returning to the environment vast quantities of waste products. The damages are already huge and are on a path to be ruinous in the future. So, a fundamental question facing societies today—perhaps the fundamental question—is how can the operating instructions for the modern world economy be changed so that economic activity both protects and restores the natural world. With increasingly few exceptions, modern capitalism is the operating system of the world economy."[4]

In *The Bridge at the Edge of the World*, I summarized my conclusions in six points:

- The vast expansion of economic activity that occurred in the twentieth century and continues today is the predominant (but not the only) cause of the environmental decline that has occurred to date. Yet, the world economy, now increasingly integrated and globalized, is poised for unprecedented growth. The engine of this growth is modern capitalism.

• A mutually reinforcing set of forces associated with today's capitalism combine to yield economic activity inimical to environmental sustainability. This result is partly the consequence of an ongoing political default—a failed politics—that not only perpetuates widespread market failure—all the nonmarket environmental costs that no one is paying—but exacerbates this market failure with deep and environmentally perverse subsidies. The result is that our market economy is operating on wildly wrong market signals.

• The upshot is that societies now face environmental threats of unprecedented scope and severity, with the possibility of various catastrophes, breakdowns, and collapses looming as distinct possibilities, especially as environmental issues link with social inequities and tensions, resource scarcity, and other issues.

• Today's mainstream environmentalism, as I described in the previous chapter, has proven insufficient in dealing with current challenges and is not up to coping with the larger challenges ahead.

• The momentum of the current system is so great that only powerful forces will alter the trajectory. Potent measures are needed that address the root causes of today's destructive growth and transform economic activity into something environmentally benign and restorative.

• In short, most environmental deterioration is a result of systemic failures of the capitalism that we have today, and long-term solutions must seek transformative change in the key features of this contemporary capitalism.[5]

As with *Red Sky at Morning*, the larger part of *The Bridge at the Edge of the World* is concerned not with identifying the problems but with pointing to the solutions. In the case of *The Bridge*, most of the actions I urge are focused on changing our current system of political economy.

My analysis was getting sharper, but I was still not happy. It is clear to anyone reading the newspapers that America is beset by multiple problems—not just environmental but also social, economic, and political. Our system of political economy is delivering bad results not only for the environment but across the whole spectrum of national life. There are more big things on our national to-do list than we have fingers and toes. A list of twenty-one is nearby, at the end of this chapter. I wanted to explore the linkages among these issues, to look more closely at our country and how we have come to find ourselves in such a sea of troubles, and to present a vision of a possible future that, while plausible, would be a place we'd be happy to have our children and grandchildren inhabit. When the Vermont Law School invited me to give a series of public lectures, my next book, *America the Possible: Manifesto for a New Economy*, was launched.

America the Possible looks more searchingly than I had previously at what went wrong in America. It argues that America got off course for primarily two reasons. "First, in recent decades we failed to build consistently on the foundations laid by the New Deal, by Franklin Roosevelt's Four Freedoms and his Second Bill of Rights, and by the United Nations' Universal Declaration of Human Rights, to which Eleanor Roosevelt contributed so much. Instead, we unleashed a virulent, fast-growing strain of corporate-consumerist capitalism. Here, I am referring not to an idealized capitalism but to the one we actually have. This system of political economy—the basic operating system of our society—rewards the pursuit of profit, growth, and power and does little to encourage a concern for people, place, and planet. 'Ours is the Ruthless Economy,' say Paul Samuelson and William Nordhaus in their text *Macroeconomics*. Indeed it is. And in its ruthlessness at home and abroad, it creates a world of wounds. As it strengthens and grows, those wounds deepen and multiply.

"Such an economy begs for restraint and guidance in the public interest—control that must be provided mainly by government. Yet the captains of our economic life, and those who have benefited disproportionately from it, have largely taken over our political life. Corporations have long been identified as our principal economic actors; they are now also our principal political actors. The result is a combined economic and political system of great power and voraciousness pursuing its own economic interests without serious concern for the values of fairness or justice or sustainability that democratic government might have provided.

"The other big and relevant development in recent American history is that our political economy evolved and gathered force in parallel with the U.S. role in the Cold War. . . . The Cold War and the rise of the American security state powerfully affected the political-economic system—strengthening the priority given to economic growth, giving rise to the military-industrial complex, and draining time, attention, and money away from domestic needs and many international challenges. This deflection of attention and resources continued with the rise of peacekeeping operations in the wake of the Cold War's end and, more recently, with the response to international terrorism.

"As a result, America now confronts a daunting array of challenges in the well-being of our people, in the conduct of our international affairs, and in the management of our planet's natural assets, at precisely the moment that it has become unimaginable that American politics as we know it will deliver the needed responses."[6]

America the Possible makes the case for driving system change so deeply that our country emerges with a new system of political economy, one programmed to routinely deliver good results for people, place, and planet. The idea of a new political economy is too big to swallow whole. System change can best be approached through a series of interacting, mutually reinforcing transformations—transformations that attack and undermine the key motivational structures of the current system, transformations that replace these old structures with new arrangements needed for a sustaining economy and a successful democracy.

As I wrote in *America the Possible*, I believe the following transformations hold the key to moving to a new political economy. We can think of each as a transition from today to tomorrow.

- *The market*: from near laissez-faire to powerful market governance in the public interest; from dishonest prices to honest ones and from unfair wages to fair ones; from commodification to reclaiming the commons, the things that rightfully belong to all of us;
- *The corporation*: from shareholder primacy to stakeholder primacy, from one ownership and profit-driven model to new business models and to economic democracy and public scrutiny of major investment decisions;

- *Economic growth*: from growth fetish to post-growth society, from mere GDP growth to growth in social and environmental well-being and democratically determined priorities;
- *Money and finance*: from Wall Street to Main Street, from money created through bank debt to money created by government; from investments seeking high financial return to those seeking high social and environmental returns;
- *Social conditions*: from economic insecurity to security, from vast inequities to fundamental fairness, from racial and other invidious discrimination to just treatment of all groups;
- *Indicators*: from GDP ("grossly distorted picture") to accurate measures of social and environmental health and quality of life;
- *Consumerism*: from consumerism and affluenza to sufficiency and mindful consumption, from more to enough;
- *Communities*: from runaway enterprise and throwaway communities to vital local economies, from social rootlessness to rootedness and solidarity;
- *Dominant cultural values*: from having to being, from getting to giving, from richer to better, from separate to connected, from apart from nature to part of nature, from near-term to long-term;
- *Politics*: from weak democracy to strong, from creeping corporatocracy and plutocracy to true popular sovereignty;
- *Foreign policy and the military*: from American exceptionalism to America as a normal nation, from hard power to soft, from military prowess to real security.[7]

Here's the good news: we are already seeing the proliferation of innovative actions along these lines, particularly at the local level: sustainable communities, transition towns, local living economies, sustainable and regenerative agriculture, new regional and organic food systems, and community investment institutions. We are also seeing the spread of innovative business models that prioritize community and environment over profit and growth—including social enterprises, for-benefit business, and co-ops of several types—as well as numerous campaigns for fair wages, worker rights, and pro-family policies. Together with new community-oriented and earth-friendly lifestyles, these initiatives provide inspirational models of how things might work in a new political economy devoted to sustaining human and natural communities. They are bringing the future into the present.

In thinking about the need for transformation when writing *America the Possible*, I had to develop a "theory of change"—how transformative change can happen. The theory affirms the centrality of hope and hope's victory over despair. It locates the plausibility of hope in knowing that many people will eventually rise up and fight for the things that they love; knowing that history's constant is change, including deep, systemic changes; and knowing that we understand enough to begin the journey, to strike out in the right directions, even if the journey's end is a place we have never been. The theory embraces the seminal role of crises in waking us from the slumber of routine and in shining the spotlight on the failings of the current order of things. It puts great stock in transformative leadership that can point beyond the crisis to something better. The theory adopts the view that systemic changes must be driven both bottom-up and top-down—from communities, businesses, and citizens deciding on their own to build the future locally as well as to develop the political muscle to adopt system-changing policies at the national and international levels. And it sees a powerful citizens' movement as a necessary spur to action at all levels.[8]

Here is how it might all come together. As conditions in our country continue to decline across a wide front, or at best fester as they are, ever-larger numbers of Americans lose faith in the current system and its ability to deliver on the values it pro claims. The system steadily loses support, leading to a crisis of legitimacy. Meanwhile, traditional crises, both in the economy and in the environment, grow more numerous and fearsome. In response, progressives of all stripes coalesce, find their voice and their strength, and pioneer the development of a powerful set of new ideas and policy proposals confirming that the path to a better world does indeed exist. Demonstrations and protests multiply, and a powerful movement for pro-democracy reform and transformative change is born. At the local level, people and groups plant the seeds of change through a host of innovative initiatives that provide inspirational models of how things might work in a new political economy devoted to sustaining human and natural communities. Sensing the direction in which the current is moving, our wiser and more responsible leaders, political and otherwise, rise to the occasion, support the growing movement for change, and frame a compelling story or narrative that makes sense of it all and provides a positive vision of a better America. It is a moment of democratic possibility.

This is, of course, a prayer. For our children and grandchildren, we must now dream up a new America and breathe life into it. The odds seem long and probably are. But as my friend Gar Alperovitz at the Democracy Collaborative often says:

"Fundamental change—indeed, radical systemic change—is as common as grass in world history."[9]

One sure sign that the search for a new political economy has begun is the way that constituencies have formed around new concepts of the economy—including the solidarity economy, the caring economy, the sharing economy, the restorative economy, the regenerative economy, the sustaining economy, the commons economy, the resilient economy, and, of course, the new economy. There is ongoing discussion of the need for a "great transition" and for a "just transition" rooted in racial, gender, and class justice. In 2013 the most searched words on the Merriam-Webster site were "capitalism" and "socialism."

Having gotten myself tolerably happy with my analysis, I've devoted much of my time in recent years working to strengthen the institutional infrastructure for change. Under whatever names, the needed transformations require institutions to promote them. Existing institutions like the Democracy Collaborative, the Institute for Policy Studies, the Tellus Institute, *Yes!* magazine, Demos, the Capital Institute, the Center for a New American Dream, Friends of the Earth, National People's Action, the Sustainable Economies Law Center, the Labor Network for Sustainability, Jobs with Justice, the National Domestic Workers Alliance, and Chelsea Green Publishing have taken up the cause, as have organizations strengthening new types of corporations such as the Business Alliance for Local Living Economies and the American Sustainable Business Council. Joining them are a series of new entities seeking to bring the many "new economy" issues and organizations together, including the New Economy Coalition and the New Economy Working Group. As I write, 120 organizations have already joined the New Economy Coalition. This is important work, and it is a privilege to be involved in it.

In parallel with these developments, another wonderful thing has happened. We are seeing the rebirth of activism in America. We are seeing it on the issue that has mattered most to me, climate change, and here I must pay my respects and state my appreciation to the remarkable Bill McKibben and the dedicated young people with him in 350.org. McKibben and friends have brought to the climate issue an unusual combination of intellectual and scientific rigor, political and media savvy, and 1960s-style in-the-streets activism that is exactly what is needed. Bill, bless him, has led this effort with grace, humor, and courage, and my hat is off.

Time is the most important variable in the equation of the future. As a spate of scientific assessments in 2014 made clear, there is not much time left to head off catastrophic climate change. The report of the Intergovernmental Panel on Climate Change implies that, if societies are to have even a two-thirds chance of holding global warming to less than +2°C, the agreed international goal, then carbon dioxide in the atmosphere can't be much more than 400 ppm by century's end. Unfortunately, we are almost there now. The current level is already 397 ppm and rising. The only responsible course for the United States is to put in place policy and other measures that will reduce US greenhouse gas emissions by 2050 to a very small fraction of today's, combined with major efforts to sequester carbon dioxide in forests, soils, and elsewhere. Regulations must be adopted that are tough enough to accomplish that emissions goal.

Here is the good news and the bad: increasingly severe climate change impacts will compel national and international responses. Our national reaction must be, as the saying goes, to walk on both feet. First, the country must take major steps now within the framework of our current system of political economy. But I doubt that the United States can go far enough and fast enough as long as we remain fixated on ramping up GDP, growing corporate profits, increasing incomes of the already well-to-do, neglecting the half of America that is just getting by, consuming endlessly, focusing only on the present moment, helping abroad only modestly, and so on. Dealing with the climate emergency in such a context is like trying to go down a very fast up escalator. So, to succeed, we need to pursue major policy reforms within the system, *and* we need to pursue equally powerful efforts to change the system itself in fundamental ways.

I was amused a few years ago reading Naomi Oreskes and Erik Conway's excellent book, *Merchants of Doubt: How a Handful of Scientists Obscured the Truth on Issues from Tobacco Smoke to Global Warming*. They make the point that the climate change deniers, by slowing action on climate change, have made far more drastic actions necessary. And then came the surprise. "Consider the case of Gus Speth. . . . After forty years as an 'inside' environmentalist, Speth has become radicalized by the world's failure to act on problems we have known about for a long time. . . . The merchants of doubt have produced just the effect they most dreaded. Southern gentlemen are now preparing to dismantle capitalism."[10]

Whether driven by climate and fossil fuel insults; poverty, low wages, and joblessness; deportation of immigrants and other family issues; treatment of women; or voter suppression, movements are now challenging key aspects of the system, seeking to drive deep change beyond incremental reform, and offering alternative visions and new paths forward. There are groups that are marching in the streets, state capitals, and local congressional offices. Others are starting to run people for office around alternative agendas. There are places where the needed research is occurring, and new coalitions are bringing diverse groups together. Strong movements can be found in other countries, and, indeed, many countries are further along than we are. These are among the grounds for hope, the reasons to believe that real change is possible. Hopefully, many who are still in the mainstream but who see the need for deep change will find ways to join this growing movement for a better world.

It's true that the more I thought and read, the more my views evolved and moved leftward. My guiding star on this journey, my recurring point of departure, has been my six grandchildren and all the other grandchildren and the fervent hope that we will have the good sense to leave them a world that is sustained and whole. Yet, while I don't mind being thought of as a "radical," that is not how I view myself. Rather, I believe my thinking is close to where Franklin Roosevelt was with his Second Bill of Rights, where Aldo Leopold and Thomas Berry were with their environmental ethics, and, in the respects that I quoted earlier, where the Southern Agrarians were in *I'll Take My Stand*. I doubt that views like mine will be thought "radical" for long. As Paul Raskin at the Tellus Institute has stressed, deep change is a pragmatic necessity; the fantasy is to think that we can continue with the status quo. I will say more about Roosevelt, Leopold, and Berry in the next and final chapter.

I hope today's young people will not worry unduly about being thought "radical" and will find ways to short circuit the long and tortuous path I took. If it seems right to you, embrace it. A wonderful group of leaders and activists who are trying to change the system for the better are building new communities in which we can all participate.

MAINSTREAM PROGRESSIVE REFORMS FOR AMERICA

- Launch a new War on Poverty aimed at lifting a sixth of our citizens out of poverty;
- Initiate programs to rebuild the middle class and to provide economic security for families with modest incomes;
- Deploy genuinely progressive taxes and other measures to raise revenues and help close the gap in incomes between rich and poor;
- Create an outstanding health care system that delivers outcomes as good as those common in Europe and at the lower costs common in Europe;
- Support educational initiatives that restore American students to the top ranks internationally and close the class and race divide in American education;
- Lower unemployment and underemployment rates to satisfactory levels, guaranteeing decent-paying jobs to all who want to participate in the labor force;
- Move the United States to the front ranks internationally in child welfare, including meaningful parental leaves and paid holidays and dramatic reductions in child abuse and in advertising targeting children;
- Provide incentives to rebuild social capital in America, including the revitalization of declining cities, encouraging American companies to stay rooted in their communities, providing compassionate

care for those who need it, recreating the "nation of joiners," and countering the rise of hate groups;

- Pass comprehensive immigration reform and deal responsibly and sensitively with illegal immigration;
- Shift away from policies that encourage consumerism and toward those that encourage long-term public and private investment in R&D, green technology, the industries of the future, modern infrastructure, environmental restoration, and community development;
- Regulate Wall Street to curb speculative activity, eliminate systemic risks, and protect investors, while building up a system of community-based financial institutions;
- Implement gun control, challenge America's gun culture, and address America's top rank in homicides;
- Address drug abuse, both legal and illegal, and correct policies that have led to America having the world's highest incarceration rate;
- Establish a monetary measure of sustainable economic welfare that is published quarterly along with GDP, and create a new system of indicators to gauge national progress;
- Using tax reform and cuts in military spending, reduce federal budgetary deficits and US international indebtedness to sustainable levels;
- Redirect America's approach to terrorism and find ways to be more effective while unwinding the post-9/11 buildup of a huge and secretive homeland security apparatus and government snooping;

- Reduce the military budget, the huge arms industry, and the network of military bases abroad, and rethink the real threats to America's national security, the training and arming of foreign military forces, the use of private contractors, and the overreliance on the military generally;

- Join with other countries in efforts to greatly strengthen international capabilities to counter neglected "unconventional" threats like the spread of infectious diseases, transnational organized crime, climate change and other global environmental challenges, humanitarian emergencies, world poverty, and human rights abuses;

- Implement comprehensive national energy and climate policies that will rapidly reduce greenhouse gas emissions, while greatly boosting energy efficiency and renewable energy;

- Prepare for resource shortages, escalating commodity and resource prices, and for the need to de-emphasize economic growth as a central pillar of national economic, budgetary, and security policy;

- Build true citizen sovereignty and political equality as well as the transparency, honesty, accountability, competence, and civility of American government and politics.

—ADAPTED FROM *AMERICA THE POSSIBLE*

Part V

What We Have Instead

In this our world

if there is meaning
we create it.

If there is community
we build it.

If there is justice
we forge it.

If there is providence
we provide it.

If there is love
we extend it.

Nothing is given
save life itself.

We have only
this speck of earth
and each other.

It is enough.

So let us pray
to fields and friends
and to the spacious sky.

—JGS

NINE

Some Things
I Think I've Learned

Nearing the end of these reflections, I want to offer some thoughts on a few things I've learned over the years, or believe I have.

One is that the main thing that gets us through life with a maximum of happiness and a modicum of success is each other. When a founder of the new field of positive psychology was asked to state as simply as he could the roots of human happiness, his answer was: "Other people." We flourish in a setting of warm, nurturing, and rewarding interpersonal relationships, and that is what I have had throughout my life at home and at work. The philosopher George Santayana quipped, "There is no cure for birth and death, save to enjoy the interval." And enjoyment of life, above all, requires companionship, affection, collaboration, support—things that we can only receive from each other, and especially in my case from Cameron. Caring for others, and being cared for by others, is what gives life meaning. In the end, I think it is just that simple.

I say it's simple, but, of course, we all too often seek to impart meaning to our lives in other ways. Almost universal is our tendency to try to find meaning at the mall. Here I refer to our consumerism, our affluenza. How wrongheaded to think that we can satisfy our nonmaterial needs with more materialism—more stuff! Many of us are familiar with Abraham Maslow's hierarchy of human needs. At the bottom of the pyramid are the material things we really do need to buy—or, even better, make ourselves—food, water, shelter, health care, education—the basics. But as we move up the pyramid, we encounter the non-material needs—friendship, belonging, intimacy, self-esteem, a sense of accomplishment. Advertisers seduce us into trying to meet these higher needs by buying stuff—cars, clothing, jewelry, beer, and so much more. Madison Avenue and its clients love consumerism precisely because it doesn't work. There is no meaning to be found at the mall. So we try again, and again. We keep buying, shop 'til we drop. But, at some level, we sense that this consumerism involves a great misdirection of life's energy. We know we're slighting the precious things that no market can provide—that truly make life worthwhile.

As the bumper sticker says, "The best things in life aren't things." So there's a revolutionary new product trying to make it in the marketplace. Not long ago, a group of young women set up a stand in a large mall to sell Nothing. They promised it was "Guaranteed not to put you in debt . . . 100 percent nontoxic . . . sweatshop-free . . . doesn't contribute to global warming . . . family-friendly . . . fun and creative!" When they refused to leave, they were arrested! Good for them. Humor is a powerful way to challenge the system—intelligent, irreverent debunking.

Another thing I've learned as I reflect over almost seven decades of remembered life is what a gift it is to have a cause—a purpose or calling, one or more, in which we can believe, something that's bigger and more important than ourselves. Of course, we are bound to experience setbacks, and times when our efforts do not seem to be working. But giving up on an important cause is not an option. Causes keep us going and galvanize our energies. Consider the principal issue I've committed myself to in the public arena—that is, to work for over thirty years to hold back the onslaught of climate change. I certainly haven't succeeded. But I have at least succeeded at trying, and, if that is not enough, it is still a lot.

Moreover, this fight is not over. In truth, it has hardly begun. Like most Americans, I love our country's boundless energy and spirited people, its natural beauty, its creativity in so many fields, its many gifts to the world, and the freedom and opportunity it has given me and others, and I don't want America ravaged by climate change. That's why on August 20, 2011, I became a jailbird for protesting the proposed Keystone XL pipeline, all 1,700 miles of it intended to carry oil from the tar sands of Alberta, Canada, to the Gulf Coast to satisfy the world's insatiable thirst for oil.

The climate struggle has been like rolling the rock up the hill only to see it roll to the bottom again. So let me mention a remarkable interpretation of Sisyphus and his rock, given to us by Albert Camus in his *The Myth of Sisyphus*. Camus says that Sisyphus was condemned by the gods to futile and hopeless labor, forever rolling a rock to the top of the mountain only to have the stone always fall back of its own weight. Sisyphus's crime was "his hatred of death, and his passion for life." But Camus finds Sisyphus "superior to his fate, . . . stronger than

Visiting Albert Camus' overgrown gravesite in Provence.

his rock." "I leave Sisyphus at the foot of the mountain," Camus writes. "[But] the struggle itself toward the heights is enough to fill a person's heart. One must imagine Sisyphus happy."[1] The struggle itself, Camus concludes, is full of meaning. So, my advice to young people today is: find *your* rock. Start pushing. You never know, it might just stay up there one day.

Perhaps the most worthy cause for any of us is taking care of children and families. What could be better? Another cause should be our communities. In America, we've had enough of throwaway cities and runaway businesses. We need to build the future locally, create intentional communities and transition towns, and launch new enterprises that are rooted and sustainable and that have a higher social purpose than profit. There is no Washington-style gridlock stopping us where we live. Follow the food.

But, of course, we cannot stop there. As I mentioned earlier, there's a long list of national and international challenges that cry out for major action in Washington. Here is what Thomas Jefferson wrote at the end of his presidency, "The care of human life and happiness . . . is the first and only legitimate object of good government." Imagine if our "leaders" in Washington focused government on "the care of human life and happiness"!

Franklin Roosevelt did. In his last State of the Union address in 1944, he called on America to accept "a second Bill of Rights under which a new basis of security and prosperity can be established for all—regardless of station, race, or creed." And Roosevelt then listed these rights:

- The right to a good job;
- The right to earn enough to provide adequate food and clothing and recreation;
- The right of every family to a decent home;
- The right to adequate medical care and the opportunity to achieve and enjoy good health;
- The right to adequate protection from the economic fears of old age, sickness, accident, and unemployment;
- The right to a good education.

Imagine these as rights! That's what the International Declaration of Human Rights, adopted by the United Nations after World War II, in fact does. Whatever the sad craziness of US politics in the current moment, the proposition that we should have these rights is not radical. They are the rights—not the hopes, not the promises, but the rights—sought for all Americans by a great president. It happened just yesterday, when I was two.

To secure these rights, and others, we all need to escape the clutches of the reigning neoliberal orthodoxy. We need to build an economy and a politics that give honest priority to people, place, and planet—rather than profit, product, and power. Whatever name this new political economy goes by, there are many inventive people working at building it today across our country. As Rebecca Solnit has written, "the grounds for hope are in the shadows, in the people who are inventing the world while no one looks."[2]

It is certainly time for a deeper critique of why our economy is not working for people, place, or planet. George Bernard Shaw famously remarked that all progress depends on being unreasonable. It's time for a large amount of civic unreasonableness. As Frederick Douglass observed in the fight against slavery, "Power concedes nothing without a demand." To protest because we care for our country is an act of high patriotism.

Thinking about protests, here is a conversation that I imagine having with a friend:

The situation today is utterly hopeless. And therein lies the hope.

You're writing again. But in riddles now.

Yes, writing. Icarus, my old friend, has come to visit me again.

But the riddle?

The America we have known is in steep decline. But the failing of the old America can open the door for something new and better to be born, a new America.

Something new and better?

Well, not entirely new. Something spun from the best of who we were, and are and can be—something fine, well worth having.

That would be nice. But is it "can" or "will"?

Only can. Between can and will there is the bifurcation. At that point, the crisis point, the path forks, and things could get a lot worse or a lot better.

What will make the difference?

You know as well as I. Preparation. Vision. Struggle. Sacrifice. It's up to us.

Sacrifice?

Like the civil rights movement and the fight against apartheid. They put it all on the line.

And they won.

They did.

Well then, I'll see you at the bifurcation.

The cause at the broadest level is the need to care for our planet and for our children and grandchildren and all future generations who will inhabit it. The brilliant governor from Illinois Adlai Stevenson spoke to our planetary future in his last speech in 1965: "We travel together, passengers in a little spaceship, . . . preserved from annihilation only by the care, the work, and, I will say, the love we give our fragile craft." Today we know that caring for our fragile craft requires much deeper change than we imagined a few decades ago.

Caring for this earth must extend to all the life that evolved here with us. It does not matter, for example, whether we think a particular species is important or a natural area beautiful. We did not create it and we do not own it. It has intrinsic value. Nature has rights. The cultural historian and visionary Thomas Berry observed that humans had created the concept of rights—and then had given them all to themselves. Aldo Leopold saw plainly and wrote beautifully that the ethics by which we live must extend to caring for the land and all the life on it. In *A Sand County Almanac* he wrote, "A thing is right when it tends to preserve the integrity, stability, and beauty of the biotic community. It is wrong when it tends otherwise."[3]

In his "Introduction" to *A Sand County Almanac*, Kenneth Brower writes that Leopold's shack "sits just above a sandy flood channel of the Wisconsin River, at a fork in the evolution of our regard for the land." One lovely fall day not long ago I made my pilgrimage to Leopold's shack. I sat on a bench there for a while, in awe of his accomplishments. Leopold reminds us of the importance of place, the lasting reservoirs of meaning that we inhabit. Place is powerful; that is another thing I've learned.

Cameron and I have moved north four times, each time further up the Eastern Seaboard, to the point that we are now just shy of Canada. Places are shaped by their histories. As Faulkner said, "The past is never dead. It's not even past." Our fine neighbors here in central Vermont, the Roots, have been here for nine generations, since the town of Strafford was founded. Our stories are so very different. One might think Cameron and I would be terribly out of place. But here is the revelation: not since Orangeburg in 1960 have we felt so much at home as we do here in Vermont. It is not merely that we have been welcomed warmly, or that we like Vermont's politics (as much as one can like any politics), or that the state is strikingly beautiful. It is those things, but it is also the startling realization that we have found here a place close kin to the South for which we hoped and dreamed.

Can we look again at what Louis Rubin said about Southern life, writing in the late 1950s? He describes a people "that did not place its reliance upon the material goods of life, but upon the values of individuality, self-reliance, the community arts, a life which did not allow getting and spending to interfere with leisurely, relaxed living. The way of life which permitted a man to enjoy himself, to know the satisfaction of being something more than a cog in a machine. . . . At its heart was an historical sense of life, an instinctive realization that man was not a creature of chance and the moment. It was a life that emphasized the right relationship of man to nature and the essential dependence of man on nature. It was a life of the spirit as well as the flesh, which provided in its makeup for recognition of the values of the spirit."

That's about how one might describe Vermont, as robust a description as any such generalization. Many in Vermont would see themselves in this description, in their habits of thought and their aspirations for themselves and their families. The big change one would have to make would be to delete the part about "leisurely, relaxed living." Vermonters are a hardworking lot and determined to get a good job done. I was on our small Vermont hill when Hurricane Irene came through. Cameron was in Washington, D.C., helping with grandchildren. Vermont, as many will remember, got tons of rain. Countless roads and bridges were washed out, towns isolated, and covered bridges carried away downstream. In its wake Vermonters quietly got out their trucks, tractors, plows, and backhoes, huddled, made a few plans, and started rebuilding their communities, expecting nothing but what they had before. There were giant gashes that would take a year or more to fix, but within a few days of Irene, Vermonters had cared for each other and fixed most of the damage. We were quietly functional again. I walked down our hill when the rains finally stopped and found a stretch of our road totally washed out. By the following day, it was repaired.

Of course the state is not perfect. Vermont has the second lowest percentage of minorities in the United States, and it could benefit from a more diverse population. But I do believe that we have settled into a place that has a sense of community, a resonance with nature, an embrace of values beyond materialism, and other admirable qualities worth promoting North and South.

Still, there is some part of Cameron and me devoted to South Carolina and the South. We have many relatives and friends there, and we treasure them. I no longer carry a torch for the South, but I know that that heritage is part of me. We decamp Vermont every year when the weather gets really bad here in early February and spend two to three months near Charleston. When there, we always drive over to Rockville and walk around under the live oak canopy that covers the lovely village. From the veranda of the old structure where dances are held each year on hot summer nights, looking down the last stretch of the Edisto you can see Seabrook Island where beyond a patch of maritime forest is Camp St. Christopher, still there, and beyond it, wrapping around to the front beach where we walked with the bishop, is now not the domain of wild nature of 1960 but the exclusive and very gated Seabrook Island Club with its large houses, townhomes, restaurants, and golf courses, a place as transformed as our country.

My friend Betsy Taylor recently sent me a remark from the always quotable George Bernard Shaw. It seems a good note on which to conclude: "This is the true joy of life, being used up for a purpose recognized by yourself as a mighty one." That has the ring of truth to me. I have had causes that are mighty, and still do. I am getting toward used up, though not there yet. And I do now feel a sense of personal joy, despite my many shortcomings and pratfalls and despite my worries about the world's many problems. The causes that have found me are good ones, and I believe I have given them my best efforts. There's a real satisfaction there, and joy also with Cameron, our family, and friends.

We must hold fast to our dreams. They underlie all our causes. We do desperately need a new American Dream—a dream of an America where the pursuit of happiness is sought not in more getting and spending but in the growth of human solidarity, real democracy, and devotion to the public good; where the average person is empowered to achieve his or her human potential; where the benefits of economic activity are widely and equitably shared; where the environment is sustained for current and future generations; and where the virtues of simple living, community self-reliance, good fellowship, and respect for nature predominate. These American traditions may not always prevail today, but they are not dead. They await us, and indeed they are today being awakened across our great country.[4]

America, Clive James wrote, is still unfolding from its dream.

Notes

2.
Things Fall Apart

1. Eugene Robinson, *Disintegration: The Splintering of Black America* (New York: Anchor Books, 2010), 39–43.
2. William D. Workman Jr., *The Case for the South* (New York: Devin-Adair, 1960), vii, 164–165, 170, 188–189, 211–212, 217–218.
3. James McBride Dabbs, *The Southern Heritage* (New York: Alfred A. Knopf, 1958), 268–270.
4. The Mike Wallace Interview, Guest: James McBride Dabbs, August 31, 1958, at http://www.hrc.utexas.edu/multimedia/video/2008/wallace/dabbs_james_mcbride.html.
5. W. J. Cash, *The Mind of the South* (New York: Vintage, 1941), 439–440.

3.
Orangeburg 1968

1. Mark Kurlansky, *1968: The Year That Rocked the World* (New York: Random House, 2005), 380.
2. Jack Bass and W. Scott Poole, *The Palmetto State: The Making of Modern South Carolina* (Columbia, SC: University of South Carolina Press, 2009), 93–95.
3. John Herbers, "Races Far Apart in Carolina City," *New York Times,* October 20, 1963, 84.
4. Jack Bass, "Documenting the Orangeburg Massacre," *Nieman Reports,* Fall 2003, 8–11.
5. Jack Bass and Jack Nelson, *The Orangeburg Massacre*, rev. ed. (Macon, GA: Mercer University Press, 2002), 212.
6. Jack Shuler, *Blood and Bone: Truth and Reconciliation in a Southern Town* (Columbia, SC: University of South Carolina Press, 2012), 6, 25, 155, 199–200, 202.

4.

South and Nation

1. Marian Wright Edelman, *Lanterns: A Memoir of Mentors* (New York: Perennial, 1999), xviii.

2. Louis D. Rubin, "An Image of the South," in Louis D. Rubin and James J. Kilpatrick, *The Lasting South* (Chicago: Henry Regnery, 1957), 14.

3. Cited in Peter Applebome, *Dixie Rising* (New York: Harcourt Brace, 1996–7), 351.

4. Charles L. Black Jr., "Paths to Desegregation," *New Republic*, October 21, 1957, 15.

5. C. Vann Woodward, *The Burden of Southern History* (New York: Mentor, 1968), 18–22.

6. James C. Cobb, *Away Down South: A History of Southern Identity* (New York: Oxford, 2005), 318.

7. Ibid., 318, 322–323. See also John Egerton, *The Americanization of Dixie: The Southernization of America* (New York: Harper's Magazine Press, 1974).

8. Peter Applebome, *Dixie Rising* (New York: Harcourt Brace, 1996–7), 8.

9. Ronald Brownstein, "How the South Rose Again," *The American Prospect*, January 17, 2006.

10. Donald Davidson et al., *I'll Take My Stand* (Baton Rouge: Louisiana State University, 1930 and 2006).

11. Aldo Leopold, *A Sand County Almanac* (New York: Oxford, 1949), vii–ix, and letter to William Vogt dated January 25, 1946.

12. Wendell Berry, "The Agrarian Standard," *Orion*, Summer, 2002.

13. Courtney White, *Grass, Soil, Hope: A Journey Through Carbon Country* (White River Junction, VT: Chelsea Green, 2014), 186–189.

5.

Reflections on a Résumé

1. Wen Stephenson, "Gus Speth: 'Ultimate Insider' Goes Radical," *Grist*, September 17, 2012, http://grist.org/climate-energy/gus-speth-ultimate-insider-goes-radical/.

2. David Burnham, "Washington and Business: The Officials Appointed by Carter," *New York Times*, December 1, 1977.

3. George M. Woodwell et al., "The Carbon Dioxide Problem: Implications for Policy in the Management of Energy and Other Resources," A Report to the Council on Environmental Quality, July 1979.

4. National Research Council, Climate Research Board, "Carbon Dioxide and Climate: A Scientific Assessment" (Washington, DC: National Academy of Sciences, 1979), viii.

5. Philip Shabecoff, "U.S. Study Warns of Extensive Problems from Carbon Dioxide Pollution," *New York Times*, January 14, 1981, A13.

6. Craig N. Murphy, *The United Nations Development Programme: A Better Way?* (New York: Cambridge, 2006), 264–265.

7. Ibid., 294.

8. John Goshko, "Annan To End U.S. Hold on Key U.N. Post," *Washington Post*, April 20, 1999.

9. Judith Miller, "Outgoing U.N. Development Chief Berates U.S.," *New York Times*, April 30, 1999.

10. "American Leaving U.S. Development Post," *New York Times*, September 15, 1998.

6.
The Greening

1. John H. Adams and Patricia Adams, *A Force for Nature* (San Francisco: Chronicle Books, 2010), 22–23.

2. Charles Reich, *The Greening of America* (New York: Random House, 1970), 18.

3. Paul Ehrlich, Anne Ehrlich, and John Holdren, *Human Ecology: Problems and Solutions* (San Francisco: W. H. Freeman, 1973), 259–274.

4. Barry Commoner, *The Closing Circle* (New York: Alfred A. Knopf, 1971), 255–275.

5. Jean Giono, *The Man Who Planted Trees* (White River Junction, VT: Chelsea Green Publishing Company, 1985), 3.

7.
Environmentalism at the Crossroads

1. Frederick Buell, *From Apocalypse to Way of Life* (New York: Routledge, 2004), 3–4.

Notes

2. James Gustave Speth, *The Bridge at the Edge of the World: Capitalism, the Environment and Crossing from Crisis to Sustainability* (New Haven: Yale University Press, 2008), chapters 3 and 11.

8.

"'Ultimate Insider' Goes Radical"

1. Wen Stephenson, "Gus Speth: 'Ultimate Insider' Goes Radical," *Grist*, September 17, 2012, http://grist.org/climate-energy/gus-speth-ultimate -insider-goes-radical/.
2. James Gustave Speth, *Red Sky at Morning: America and the Crisis of the Global Environment* (New Haven: Yale University Press, 2004), 96–97.
3. Ibid., 116.
4. James Gustave Speth, *The Bridge at the Edge of the World: Capitalism, the Environment, and Crossing from Crisis to Sustainability* (New Haven: Yale University Press, 2008), 6–7.
5. Ibid., 8–9.
6. James Gustave Speth, *America the Possible: Manifesto for a New Economy* (New Haven: Yale University Press, 2012), 3–4.
7. Based on Speth, *America the Possible*, 10–11.
8. Speth, *America the Possible*, 14–15.
9. Gar Alperovitz, *America Beyond Capitalism* (Hoboken, NJ: John Wiley and Sons, 2005), ix.
10. Naomi Oreskes and Erik M. Conway, *Merchants of Doubt* (New York: Bloomsbury, 2010), 255.

9.

Some Things I Think I've Learned

1. Albert Camus, *The Myth of Sisyphus and Other Essays* (New York: Random House, 1955), 89–91.
2. Rebecca Solnit, *Hope in the Dark* (New York: Penguin, 2006), 164.
3. Aldo Leopold, *A Sand County Almanac* (New York: Oxford, 1949), 224–225.
4. See James Gustave Speth, "What Is the American Dream?: Dueling Dualities in the American Tradition," *Grist*, June 24, 2011, http://www .grist.org/politics/2011-06-24-what-is-the-american-dream-dueling -dualities-in-the-american-tra/.

Index

Note: JGS refers to the author, James Gustave Speth. Page numbers in *italics* refer to photographs.

196

Index

Index

Index

Index

**green
press**
INITIATIVE

Chelsea Green Publishing is committed to preserving ancient forests and natural resources. We elected to print this title on 100-percent postconsumer recycled paper, processed chlorine-free. As a result, for this printing, we have saved:

**25 Trees (40' tall and 6-8" diameter)
12 Million BTUs of Total Energy
2,135 Pounds of Greenhouse Gases
11,583 Gallons of Wastewater
775 Pounds of Solid Waste**

Chelsea Green Publishing made this paper choice because we and our printer, Thomson-Shore, Inc., are members of the Green Press Initiative, a nonprofit program dedi-.cated to supporting authors, publishers, and suppliers in their efforts to reduce their use of fiber obtained from endangered forests. For more information, visit: www.greenpressinitiative.org.

Environmental impact estimates were made using the Environmental Defense Paper Calculator. For more information visit: www.papercalculator.org.

About the Author

JAMES GUSTAVE "GUS" SPETH is the former dean of the Yale School of Forestry and Environmental Studies, founder and president of the World Resources Institute, and cofounder of the Natural Resources Defense Council. He has also been administrator of the United Nations Development Programme, chair of the UN Development Group, professor of law at Georgetown University, and chair of the US Council on Environmental Quality in the Carter administration. He currently teaches at Vermont Law School and is a senior fellow at the Democracy Collaborative, where he is co-chair of the Next System Project. He is also distinguished senior fellow with Demos, associate fellow with the Tellus Institute, and the recipient of numerous environmental awards. His previous books include *America the Possible: Manifesto for a New Economy* and the award-winning *The Bridge at the Edge of the World: Capitalism, the Environment, and Crossing from Crisis to Sustainability* and *Red Sky at Morning: America and the Crisis of the Global Environment*.

He lives in Strafford, VT, with his wife, Cameron.

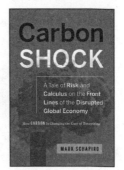